This book is due for return on or before the last date shown below.

KICKING AGAINST TRADITION

A Career in Women's Football

Wendy Owen

TEMPUS

To Cathy and Rhian

First published 2005

Tempus Publishing Limited
The Mill, Brimscombe Port,
Stroud, Gloucestershire, GL5 2QG
www.tempus-publishing.com

© Wendy Owen, 2005

British Library Cataloguing in Publication Data.
A catalogue record for this book is available from the British Library.

ISBN 0 7524 3427 6

Typesetting and origination by Tempus Publishing Limited
Printed in Great Britain

Contents

Acknowledgements   6
Foreword by Hazel Irvine   7
Preface   9

1   Getting Started   11
2   Hitting the Big Time   20
3   On Tour with England   44
4   Media Coverage   70
5   Off to the USA   75
6   Coaching Football in England 1973-1992   102
7   A New Era   119
8   Back to the Future   136

Notes   149
Appendix I: International Playing Career   151
Appendix II: Key Dates in Women's Football
    in the Post-1966 Era   152
Index   155

Acknowledgements

I would like to express my sincere thanks and gratitude to the following: my family (Mum, Dad, Chris, Tim and Viv) without whose continued love and support none of my achievements in football and in life would have been possible; Cathy and Rhian, whose love and patience enabled the book to be completed; my good friends Gillian and Paul Rossiter for always being there in my hour of need; my uncle, Edward Knight, for sharing his memories of our family and its sporting achievements; Colin and Geraldine French and Bernadette and Bernard Caswell for providing information and photographs from the Thame Ladies' years; Patricia Gregory for providing me with information about the Women's Football Association and the first England team; my ex-England colleagues Julia Brunton (née Manning), Carol Thomas (née McCune), Elaine Badrock, Sylvia Gore and Sue Lopez for sharing memories and photographs of our experiences with the national team; Kelly Simmons, Bev Ward, Rachel Pavlou, Graham Keeley and Donna McIvor at the FA for providing me with a valuable insight into recent FA development strategies for women's football; Faye White and Kelly Smith for sharing their experiences as players in the current England team; Stewart Fowlie from BUSA for information about university women's football; Francisco Marcos, Jim Kaufman, Roley Howard and Rodney Marsh for filling in the gaps concerning my USA adventures; Mick Smoothey, Andy Roderick, Melissa Lee, Val Stephens, John Johnstone, Fiona Miley, Josie Clifford and Geraldine Lynch for provision of either information or photographs that contributed to various other sections of the book; Sol River for his invaluable advice in the early stages of writing the book; Holly Bennion and all the team at Tempus Publishing.

Every effort has been made to trace the copyright of images used in this book. If any copyright has been inadvertently infringed, please contact the publishers.

Foreword
by Hazel Irvine

Let's make one thing clear. Wendy Owen is not Michael's Mum!

He's an England striker. She was a central defender for her country. Indeed as part of the very first England women's squad, Wendy Owen was a pioneer. Had women's football had the same profile as the men's game she, like Michael, might also have become a recognisable role model for a generation of footballers.

Ahh, but there's the rub. When Wendy was fulfilling her international dreams in the 1970s the women's game was only just emerging from fifty years in obscurity. Female players had been banned from playing on FA pitches since 1921. (Before then, the game had become so popular during the First World War that teams such as Dick, Kerr Ladies and Manchester Corinthians played to crowds in excess of 35,000.)

So, by the time Wendy made her international debut in 1972, she and her colleagues had to put up with all of the old clichés all over again: 'What does your boyfriend think of you playing?', 'Trap it on yer chest, love...' and, of course, 'football's a man's game'.

Wendy recounts tales, both fun and frustrating, of those early days on tour with England when she gained sixteen caps for her country. Thereafter she takes us through her twenty-five-year career in coaching, where she became one of the first women to gain the FA coaching certificate and the UEFA 'B' licence. We learn of her experiences in the United States with, amongst other soccer set-ups, the Tampa Bay Rowdies. Ultimately, we follow her progress into academia as a senior lecturer in sports science and coach education. Amongst all this we hear of the potholes of prejudice and chauvinism scattered along her route.

Despite the setbacks, Wendy's competitive sprit shines through: she once dropped her shorts, handed them to her manager, and told him that if he thought he could do a better job, he should try them for size! Equally self-evident is

Owen's sheer love of football and her desire to inspire other women and girls to share her passion by taking up the game.

In my own career as a sports journalist I have been fortunate to work on some of the very first outside broadcasts of women's football, both for BBC Sport and Channel 4.

I well remember covering the 1995 Women's World Cup in Sweden in which England reached the quarter finals. I acted as presenter/reporter. Clive Tyldesley did the commentary. Ultimately the trophy was claimed by Norway after an exciting final against Germany. The whole fortnight was one long celebration of the game – the sheer exuberance of the play and the positive, attacking tactics of the teams were hugely enjoyable to watch.

Since then, fitness and skill levels in the women's game have improved even more. It's becoming ever more professional, especially in the United States, Scandinavia and Germany. In those countries football is very definitely NOT just 'a man's game'.

Happily, here in Britain, as in the USA, women's football is now the nation's fastest growing sport. We are producing young female role models for the national teams who are no longer curiosities. It's taken decades to achieve.

As a player and now as a coach, Wendy Owen has helped bring about this change. Her book is an illuminating insight into what it took to get here.

Hazel Irvine

Preface

On 15 November 1972, I took the famous walk up the tunnel and out on to the hallowed turf at Wembley Stadium as a member of the first official England women's football team. We were greeted by a bank of photographers from the national press, there to take pictures of us. This was a scenario that I had imagined many times as a young girl growing up in the late 1950s and 1960s. With football deemed to be an 'unsuitable game for women' at that time and females banned (since 1921) from playing on FA pitches, it was not, however, one that I could have actually expected to come true.

This book, among other things, tells the story of how my dream of playing football for my country became a reality. It is about much more than that, however. It is about how a whole new generation of girls and young women, inspired by the heroics of the England men's team in the 1966 World Cup, refused to be denied access to the people's game for any longer and began literally kicking against tradition. It charts our successes in breaking down the barriers, getting the rules changed, reclaiming our right of access to the nation's football pitches and finally changing attitudes and gaining acceptance from both the FA and wider society that it was okay for women to play.

Beyond my experiences as a player, the book goes on to look at my forays into the world of football coaching, both in this country and the USA. It gives some insight into the reasons why women's soccer has become so hugely successful across the Atlantic and looks at what the FA is currently doing to try to enable England's women to catch up.

Wendy Owen

one

Getting Started

I was born in 1954 in Slough, when it was still a part of Buckinghamshire. Although my parents grew up, met and married there, my mother (Joy) is English and my father (David) Welsh. This had the benefit of giving me dual nationality in sporting terms; by the age of nineteen I was very proud to have played both football for England and netball for Wales.

Our family is one with a sporting pedigree. My father is very knowledgeable and enthusiastic about a range of sports and had set up and run a successful amateur boys' football team before I was born. It was from my mother's side of the family, however, that I probably inherited my sporting genes. My uncle, Edward Knight (my mother's eldest brother) was a professional boxer and a professional endurosport motorcycle rider in the 1930s. He rode all over the continent for the Munich-based BMW team. His son, John Knight, went on to become British champion at the sport, winning three World gold medals. According to family folklore, there was also a 'Knight' who played football for Tottenham Hotspur before the First World War, although I have been unable to verify this.

I began to show my athletic prowess from the age of two, when my mother left me unattended in the back garden of our modest semi-detached house in Slough. Her back was only turned for a moment but when she re-emerged from the kitchen, I was nowhere to be seen. At first she didn't panic as the gate was firmly shut and the whole garden was surrounded by a six-foot-high fence. When a search of both the house and garden and repeated calling had yielded nothing her calm demeanour finally began to crack. She opened the gate, went out into the street and began to run up and down frantically calling my name. I know all this, not only because the story has been retold many times down the years, but also because I can remember observing it from my vantage point in the branches of our apple tree. My mother hadn't thought to look up because I don't suppose she knew of many two-year-olds who were capable of climbing trees.

By the age of three I was terrorising the boys at the local state nursery school. My place was secured with the help of our family doctor, who prescribed it in order to preserve my mother's health! I was, by all accounts, 'a bit of a handful'. Highly energetic, full of mischief and fiercely competitive, I couldn't stand to lose at anything and would throw a tantrum as soon as defeat in a family game became inevitable. On a more positive note, you could say that from an early age I was exhibiting all the necessary attributes to enable me to become a successful sportswoman.

My love of organised sports began to blossom in primary school in the early 1960s. By then we had moved from Slough to Beaconsfield in Buckinghamshire, where my father had taken up a new post as leader at the local youth club. My siblings (my older sister Viv and my younger twin brothers Chris and Tim) and I were sent to Holtspur Primary School, near Beaconsfield. It was a wonderful school with a dedicated headmaster, Mr Tame, who believed in developing pupils' talents in sports and drama as well as promoting academic excellence. The school ran teams after school and held an annual sports day, where I excelled in high jump and the three-legged race! I played netball and rounders for the school team and entered house padder tennis competitions.

School sport in this era was still run on very traditional lines, however, and football was strictly for the boys. Consequently, my passion for 'the beautiful game' was to develop and flourish outside the education system. My father was very influential in this process. He instilled a love of football in me and was keen to nurture the enthusiasm and ability that I began to demonstrate.

One of my earliest footballing memories is of England winning the World Cup in 1966. I was only twelve at the time and I am not sure how much my recollection of the key moments of that historic final has been informed by seeing them repeated over and over again in subsequent years. What I can recall clearly, however, is watching the game on the television with my Dad and the sense of euphoria in our living room when the final whistle blew. After that I began to spend hours juggling and kicking a ball around in the back garden, imagining that I was Geoff Hurst or Martin Peters (there were no female equivalents for me to idolise at that time) and my father started taking me with him to Craven Cottage to watch Fulham play.

I have some wonderful memories of 'going to the match' with my Dad in the late 1960s and early 1970s: joining up with the growing throng as we made our way along the narrow streets towards the ground; queuing at the turnstiles to be admitted, while the police horses gently guided the crowd; standing on the terraces at the Hammersmith End as one of the few females in among a host of boys and men; looking down the ground toward the unique little cottage in the corner at the opposite end that apparently used to be a cricket pavilion in Edwardian times and gave the ground its name; and waiting for our heroes to emerge from the changing rooms and run out on to the field of play.

Fulham were still in the old First Division of the Football League between 1966 and 1968 when I first became a fan. They had great players like Johnny Haynes (who was coming towards the end of his career but was a great inside forward who had captained England), George Cohen (full-back in the World Cup-winning team of 1966), Jimmy Conway (a speedy Irish winger) and Les Barrett (who also played on the wing). It wasn't just the Fulham players that we went to see, however. All the top clubs visited Craven Cottage at that time (before May 1968 when Fulham were relegated from the First Division and went into freefall, ending up in the Third!). One particular occasion that will always stand out in my mind, however, was a visit from Manchester United when a certain George Best was in the side. He was a real crowd-puller wherever he went and Craven Cottage was full to capacity that day. My Dad and I were in our usual spot in a packed Hammersmith End as George began one of his trademark runs towards the Fulham goal, which happened to be at our end. This was when excitement turned to apprehension for me. I had already been feeling pretty wedged in among the unusually large crowd but, as it surged forward in anticipation of a shot from Best, I felt the weight of bodies pushing against my ribs and almost crushing the breath out of me. Dad realised what was happening to me and other youngsters, as did the policemen at the front on the pitch. They began to help us to move forward down the terrace and lifted us out on to the pitch to safety. After that things got really thrilling because some of us were allowed to climb up to watch the game from a little way up the floodlight gantry (I am sure that that would be against the rules now!). I enjoyed a fantastic aerial view of the game from up there, which I think was won by United, although I can't recall the score.

After Fulham were relegated from the First Division in 1968, I must confess to developing divided loyalties. I still enjoyed going to games at Craven Cottage but, in 1969, I fell in love with Don Revie's crack Leeds United team, who were always being featured on *Match of the Day*. As well as tasting European glory in the Fairs Cup in 1968, they had won the First Division Championship for the first time in the 1968/69 season, beating Bill Shankly's Liverpool. I was putting myself out on a limb in supporting them, because the Leeds team was pretty unpopular in the south of England, where they were seen as rather physical and defensive. I thought that they had attacking flair too, however, and was altogether very impressed with their style of play. The squad of 1969/70 – Sprake, Harvey, Reaney, Cooper, Charlton, Yorath, Madeley, Hunter, Bremner (capt), Gray, Lorimer, Giles, Clarke, Jones, Bates, Hibbitt and Belfitt – became my heroes and role models and their names were plastered all over my school books. My particular favourites were Jack Charlton (centre half for England in the 1966 World Cup) Peter Lorimer (an attacking midfielder with a very pow-erful shot), Norman Hunter (for his ferocious tackling) and Allan Clarke (a deadly striker) but I really rated them all. I followed the team's progress closely that season and was elated when they beat Manchester United to reach the final of the FA Cup. Up until that point, however, I had only seen the team play on the television. I was absolutely over the moon when my Dad told me that he had managed to get me a cup final ticket. I was going to see them live for the first time, and at Wembley no less!

My Dad had made a big sacrifice in giving me that ticket, because it was the only one that he could secure from a group allocation that another nearby youth club had managed to attain. Consequently I went to the 1970 FA Cup final, between Leeds United and Chelsea, chaperoned by another adult that he trusted, while Dad stayed at home to watch the game on the television. The trouble was that the rest of the group that I was going with were Chelsea sup-porters. I was wearing a Leeds United scarf and a hat with a big picture of my team plastered all over it, which did make me a focus for attention when we arrived on the terraces in a Chelsea section of the ground! The fans around me were very good natured, however, and didn't seem to mind when a sixteen-year-old girl began waving a rattle and screaming for Leeds at the top of her voice.

The build-up to the game (travelling to Wembley and walking with the crowds up the Wembley Way) had been exciting and the game matched up to it. Leeds scored first via Jack Charlton, which was deserved as the team was playing very well. Just before half-time disaster struck, however, when the Leeds goalkeeper, Gary Sprake, let a fairly tame shot squirm under his body for a Chelsea equaliser. Gary could make you exasperated at times. He came from the same mould as 'keepers like Bruce Grobbelaar and David James. He dealt brilliantly with the most difficult saves but the easy ones sometimes evaded his grasp! I was pretty dejected at half-time because I felt that we should have been ahead, but at least there was still everything to play for. Leeds came out and dominated play again in the second half, with our centre forward, Mick Jones, heading a goal to put Leeds 2-1 up. This time I really thought that the cup was ours but once again Chelsea came back to score a late equaliser from a free-kick. The game finished 2-2, which meant that the final would go to a replay for the first time in fifty-eight years; there were no cruel penalty kick competi-tions to decide the winners in those days.

The atmosphere among the fans after the game was understandably subdued. It seemed really strange, however, to be walking away from Wembley with no-one shouting and celebrating. I was really down because I thought that Leeds had deserved to win, while the group that I was with were just relieved that Chelsea had lived to fight another day.

The replay took place two weeks later at Old Trafford. I watched it on television over at the youth club, which as it turned out was a bit of a mistake; everyone else was supporting Chelsea. I was really convinced that Leeds would do it this time but the gods were against us again. Leeds went ahead for what was the third time over the two games but Chelsea equalised, this time through a Peter Osgood header. Then, in injury time, Chelsea scored a goal that I shall never forget; it went in off the head of David Webb to win the cup and everyone else in the room seemed to be celebrating at my expense! I wasn't very good at taking defeat at that age and I can remember being angry and depressed about the result for weeks.

Although all the footballers that I knew of and idolised in the late 1960s and early 1970s were male, it didn't stop me wanting to emulate them and become a good performer myself. As well as watching the game, I was at the same time learning how to play it. My football skills were developed and honed through hours of practice with my younger brothers (Chris and Tim Owen) and their friends (Andy Jeffery, Bob Calow, Kevin Finlinson, David Pratt, Mick Grimsdell and Nicky House) on the green just across the road from our council house. Most nights after school, every weekend and every day of the school holidays, we would meet up to play informal games with jumpers for goalposts. We practised penalty shoot-outs and corner kicks, played one versus one games and small-sided passing and dribbling games, all without the interference of adults. Disputes over the rules were settled among ourselves. This game-related approach with minimum intervention from the coach is, interestingly, something that the Football Association are currently trying to return to when working with young players.

When it was too wet to play on the green we moved to the garage area provided for tenants, where there was a concrete surface, or persuaded my Dad to let us play five-a-side in the gym at Beaconsfield Youth Club. I was the only girl, playing among a group of boys, so I developed speed and toughness (incidentally, over the years the very successful Norwegian Women's international team has trained against men for this very reason). I was accepted by the group because, according to my father, I was better than the boys. The only problem I ever had in this respect was when a new boy moved into the area and came to join our group. He objected to playing with a girl and somehow managed to move the others to a vote on whether or not I should be allowed to continue to participate. Fortunately, everyone apart from him voted for me and he was told in no uncertain terms that I stayed and he could go if he didn't like it. Thanks lads!

Although my friends and immediate family were very supportive towards me playing football, I was very aware that in wider society it was not considered to be a very suitable game for girls. Relatives and other visitors to our house would often remark about me in my hearing, 'Oh, isn't she a little tomboy.' I am sure that this was not intended in any derogatory way. It did, however, convey to me the message that, by running around on the green kicking a football, I wasn't behaving like a real girl. I wasn't going to let this put me off playing though. I was strong-willed and independently minded, and above all loved the thrill of juggling, dribbling and kicking a football, with a real passion. At that point in my life, I didn't know of any other girls who played the game, but as long as I could, I didn't mind being different.

When I progressed on to high school, I discovered that some of my school-teachers were not particularly enamoured with my enthusiasm for the sport either. My form teacher (who shall remain nameless) was particularly discouraging to the point of trying to stop me from playing. She asked my father to come into school to discuss the matter with her. When my Dad came home he told us that she had advised him to encourage me to give up playing football as it was a distraction to my studies and wouldn't get me anywhere. Luckily both my parents were very supportive and believed in encouraging all of their children in whatever they wanted to do. They had no intention of following my teacher's advice and I was allowed to carry on with my football. In subsequent years, whenever I was playing or coaching abroad, I used to send that teacher a postcard from wherever I was, so that she could see just how far the game had got me!

My traditional girls' grammar school was in fact not really ready for me, or me for it. I was like a square peg in a round hole. I was so full of energy that I found it difficult to sit still in lessons and was always in trouble with the teachers. One subject that I almost always behaved in however was physical education. I lived for these lessons and for lunchtime practices and after-school and Saturday morning matches. I excelled in a variety of sports (representing the school in netball, hockey, tennis and athletics, and Bucks County Schools at netball and hockey) and had ambitions to be a PE teacher. My first sporting love was always football though, but in the 1960s this was not part of the curricular or extra-curricular programme for girls in schools.

With no opportunity to play the sport in school I found myself, at the age of fourteen, struggling to find a way to graduate into organised competitive football. My brothers and the other lads in our group had formed a team called 'The Avenue', named after the street where we had grown up and played our football together. My father had been persuaded to manage them and entered the team in the Slough Boys' League. I was, of course, desperate to play too and incensed at being relegated to the sidelines. Competitive mixed football wasn't, however (and still isn't after the age of eleven), sanctioned by the Football Association and organised league football for girls and women was yet to take off. Although it seems hard to believe now, with all that the Football Association is currently doing to promote the women's game in this country, in 1968 the situation was very different. There was still a long-standing FA rule in place that barred women from playing on affiliated pitches and banned registered referees from officiating at women's matches! This rule dated back to 1921, when it was brought in to curb the hugely popular charity women's football matches that were playing to large crowds on professional Football League teams' grounds during and after the First World War. The official reasons for the ruling, given by the FA at the time, were that, firstly, football was an unsuitable game for females and ought not to be encouraged, and secondly, that some of the funds from these matches were being misappropriated. It has since been suggested that the real reason for the FA's action may have had more to do with the fact that women's football was perceived as a threat to the men's game as it had become far too successful (by 1920, Dick, Kerr Ladies, a factory team from Preston in Lancashire, were reputedly playing matches to crowds of upwards of 35,000 at grounds such as Goodison Park, St James' Park and Stamford Bridge). Whatever the truth of the matter, the rule made it very difficult for women's teams to find pitches to play on and referees willing to officiate. This effectively sounded the death knell for the initial boom in women's football in England during the early 1900s (Dick, Kerr Ladies did in fact manage to continue playing right up until 1965 but the number of teams playing the game did decline considerably). The FA ruling was still having an impact on girls like me nearly fifty years on but, as luck would have it, I just happened to be trying to get started in organised, competitive football at the time when things were set to change.

Angry at not being allowed to play with the boys, I pestered my father into starting a girls' football team at Beaconsfield Youth Club. Dad was in fact instrumental in the setting up of a South Bucks Youth Clubs League, one of the first of its kind, where girls' teams from other youth clubs in the local area (such as Britwell, Amersham, Chesham and Aylesbury) played friendly matches against one another on an ad hoc basis. Playing friendly matches with unregistered referees on pitches within the grounds of youth clubs, hospitals, military bases and the like was actually the way that many girls' teams got started around this time, in what turned out to be a new nationwide wave of enthusiasm from girls and women who wanted to play football following the success of the England men's team in the 1966 World Cup. These pitches, unlike many local parks pitches, did not come under the jurisdiction of the Football Association, so it was a way around the ban.

Although I was pleased to be getting my first taste of eleven-a-side football, I was very frustrated, as the competition in the girls' youth club league was well below my standard. After all, up to this point, I had played all my football with and against boys. It was not uncommon in these early fixtures for me to be able to pick the ball up in defence and dribble through the opposition, down the full length of the pitch, to score at the other end! Had I continued to play at this level I would never have realised my dream. Fortunately my lucky break was just around the corner. This came on the day that the girls from Thame (in Oxfordshire) came to Beaconsfield to play against us. It was summer 1970 and the start of a fantastic two years of football that saw me go on to play against some of the best women's teams in the country, and culminated in my selection to attend the trials for the first ever England women's football squad.

The team that was to become the highly successful Thame Ladies team started life in 1969 as the Thame Youth Club Girls' team. In common with my Beaconsfield team (and indeed many of the other girls' teams that were springing up at that time) it was started by fathers in response to the clamouring from their daughters to be given the opportunity to play football. Colin French had been running the boys' team at Thame Youth Club, assisted by Don Merrilees. Colin's sixteen-year-old twin daughters Sandra and Sheila French, Don's daughter Tina Merrilees and their football-mad friend Sally Walker all belonged to the youth club and wanted to play football. Like me, they were not allowed to play at their secondary school, where they were told off for kicking the ball instead of throwing it! Colin and Don listened to their pleas and started a girls' team at the youth club. They put an advert in the local paper asking girls who wanted to play football to contact them, and were inundated with replies. As there were not many other teams operating in the area at the time, most of the good young players from Thame and its outlying villages were recruited into the new team. These included, among others, Corrine and Gloria Eele (Thame), Jayne Hopkins and Bernadette Caswell (Haddenham), Shirley Entwistle (Shabbinton) and Yvonne Blaine (Brill).

Although a relatively new and young team, when Thame came to Beaconsfield to play against us they were already a force to be reckoned with. They were enjoying their first competitive season in the newly formed Oxfordshire League, in which they finished runners-up and won the President's Cup. My team, which was made up of relative novices, was soundly beaten. Although I never enjoyed losing, I can remember being very excited and impressed by the whole experience of that game. I had never before seen, let alone played against, any girls who had the football skills that the Thame players demonstrated. Luckily, my performance had not gone unnoticed either. The then Thame manager, Colin French, recalls being particularly amazed by my long throw-ins, which caught their team by surprise. In his words, 'I couldn't believe it when I saw you throw at Beaconsfield, you could throw as well as any bloke.' Colin and Don spotted my all-round potential as a player that day and later approached my father and asked him if I would like to come and join their team. That really was the crucial turning point in my footballing career!

Thanks to the support of both my father and the assistant leader at Beaconsfield Youth Club (Val Stephens, née Bennett) who used to share the task of ferrying me backwards and forwards on the forty-mile round trip from Beaconsfield to Thame every weekend, I now had the opportunity to begin to compete at a good standard of football. This was to be very influential in both my development as a player and the realisation of my dream to play for my country.

I joined the team towards the end of the 1969/70 season (at the age of sixteen) at a time when both Thame Ladies and women's football in England were about to take off. The Women's Football Association, which was to organise and govern the sport for the next twenty-four years and set-up the first official England team had been formed in November 1969 with forty-four clubs as initial members.[1] Although yet to be officially recognised by the FA, the WFA had already been influential in persuading the governing body to rescind its 1921 rule on access to pitches and referees for women's games. This had taken place at the beginning of the year (January 1970)[2] and was to be crucial in enabling girls like myself to start playing organised competitive football.

Thame Ladies was an up-and-coming team with good young players that, over the next two seasons (1970/71 and 1971/72) would affiliate to the WFA and progress to play in reputable league and cup competitions against other good teams and players from all over the country. I was very fortunate to be in the right place at the right moment, to be able to get involved in this and get my chance of hitting the big time.

two

Hitting the Big Time

THE BUTLIN'S CUP: AUGUST/SEPTEMBER 1970

The first time that I turned out in the red and white colours of Thame Ladies was to play in the Butlin's Cup. This was a competition inspired and sponsored by Hughie Green, presenter of the popular ITV television quiz game show *Opportunity Knocks*. As a result of a challenge laid down by a female contestant on the programme, who happened to be a keen footballer, Hughie Green was prompted to go on to promote the women's game through sponsoring a 'ladies television football league' in association with Butlin's holiday camps and the *Daily Mirror*. This involved club teams from different areas throughout England and Scotland travelling to various Butlin's camps to play matches once a fortnight in the summer/autumn season. The competition progressed through zone and inter-zone finals, before culminating in National (All-England and All-Scotland) and International (English Champions *v.* Scottish Champions) finals.

The whole affair provided good entertainment for the Butlin's holiday-makers and also for the television audiences of *Opportunity Knocks*, who were kept informed of proceedings by Hughie Green. On one particular show, he said to his glamorous hostess, 'if any of the teams are short, Monica Rose, you go out and get yourself a pair of football boots!' This all did wonders for the promotion of the women's game.

Thame entered the competition during the summer of 1970, in its second season of operation. By this time, the original squad had been bolstered by the addition of players from clubs outside the Thame area. As well as me, these included Sue Goodwin and Alison East from Oxford and Margaret (Paddy) McGroarty and Maureen Dawson from Buckingham. The Buckingham girls joined Thame because, while most of their team were playing just for the fun of it, they wanted to play serious competitive football in the Butlin's Cup. In my case, I was in it for a bit of both! Deadly serious about my football but also a fun-loving joker, playing for Thame offered me the perfect combination. The team had already experienced some success and was 'going places' but it was also full of young players like myself (our team's average age was around eighteen) who were game for a laugh.

We had a lot of fun playing in the Butlin's competition. The whole experience of travelling by coach to the Butlin's (Clacton) holiday camp once a fortnight generated a great sense of camaraderie and team spirit, and proved a great way for me to quickly get to know the other girls in the squad.

As part of the sponsorship deal we had vouchers for complimentary meals in the communal dining room. One thing that sticks in my memory about this was that everything on the menu always seemed to be green! There was green cabbage for the main course and green jelly and green ice cream for dessert. On one occasion this was complimented by a plague of greenfly in the camp. It was like walking through a swarm of locusts. You couldn't open your eyes or your mouth, or they flew right in. We had to play football under these conditions, as the competition round had to be completed. We won the game but were finding the little pests in all sorts of places for most of the following week! The only thing that wasn't green about Butlin's was the football pitch. This was devoid of grass, bumpy and rock hard (it was advisable to avoid falling over on it whenever possible). We did manage to play good football on it, however, and were soon making excellent progress in the tournament.

After beating Legs United 9–0 (their name suggests that, unlike us, not all the teams were taking the game that seriously!) and Clacton Ladies 3–2 in the early rounds, we met a team called Woolpit Bluebirds from Stowmarket (Suffolk) in the London and South-East England zone final. We were all very psyched up for this game, which was probably reflected in the fact that our inside right, Jayne Hopkins, scored straight from the kick-off. Tall and skinny, with long blond hair, Jayne was an excellent striker with a powerful shot. In both her build and her style of play, she resembled Allan Clarke from the successful Leeds United team of the 1970s that contained my heroes and role models. Shortly after Jayne had scored, Margaret (Paddy) McGroarty added a second. Paddy was one of the girls who had joined Thame from the Buckingham team. (She was in the army and stationed at nearby Bicester. In a former life she had been a novice nun!) At twenty-six, she was much older and more experienced than the rest of us, having previously played for the Hooverettes from Glasgow, one of the top Scottish club sides. She was a versatile utility player, who was given a free role in our team, operating from midfield and out towards the right wing (rather like David Beckham's role at Real Madrid). Paddy was only small in stature (she used to call me 'Big Wendy' because of our great height difference) but she had great strength and fantastic skills. Although a Scot, she went on to play in the first England team with me and became known as 'the George Best of women's football'. Just before half-time she went on one of her trademark mazy runs, beating three defenders in the process, to set-up an easy tap in for Jayne Hopkins to score her second goal of the game. When the whistle went for half-time we were a comfortable 3-0 up. The Bluebirds pulled a goal back just after the interval but we still managed to cruise to victory, winning the match three goals to one.

We were now through to the inter-zone final where we would face the winners of the South-West and Western England zone final. At this point, the local press began to sit up and take notice of our achievement. A match report of the Bluebirds game appeared in the local paper, together with all our names and a team photograph. This was very exciting for us as players and also started to generate interest within the local community as we were now only one game away from appearing in the All-England Final, to be played at Hendon Football Club in London.

More than fifty supporters made the trip to Clacton to see us beat Niton Dollies, from the Isle of Wight, 9-0 in the All-England semi-final. Some of them came just for the day out or because they thought that seeing women playing football would be a bit of a laugh. The latter was also true of some of the members of the crowd that we used to draw for home games. Bernie Caswell's father (Bernard) who was a regular on the sidelines recalls that these people (mostly men) had to eat humble pie when they saw how well we could play. Some of the initial sceptics were even overheard making the observation that we were good enough to beat many of the male youth teams in the Thame area!

In football terms, the semi-final was a bit of a disappointment as the opposition provided little resistance. We were 4-0 ahead by half-time and scored another five goals in the second half with no reply. I even managed to get on the score sheet! At the time, I was playing as an overlapping right full-back in a back three with the 'French twins' (Sandra French played in the centre and Sheila at left-back). I had little to do in my defensive role, but I managed to convert a penalty kick.

We grabbed the headlines the next week with a big spread in the *Thame Gazette*. It read 'Thame Girls in T.V. Cup Final' and went on, 'The incredible Thame Girls soccer team on Sunday won their way to the final of the Ladies Television Football Cup, probably the most important trophy in ladies soccer in this country.' Our semi-final win was also announced on *Opportunity Knocks* that week, with Hughie Green saying on the programme, 'Thame Ladies are not so tame, they have made the final'. For a young girl who had, only a few months earlier, been cutting a lone furrow in friendly matches for Beaconsfield Youth Club, this really was heady stuff.

As a result of our growing notoriety, we were able to make links with our local professional football club, Oxford United. One of their players, Micky

Way, a skilful inside forward, who lived in Thame and had previously played for Thame United, began to help us with our training. He did some useful circuit training and skills work with us in the run up to the final. In the week prior to the Hendon match, we were pictured in the local newspaper with both Micky Way and one of the Oxford United directors (Vic Couling) who presented us with a lucky bear mascot in United's colours. The excitement and pressure was mounting in readiness for the big day.

BUTLIN'S CUP ALL-ENGLAND FINAL: THAME LADIES v. FODEN LADIES, 20 SEPTEMBER 1970, HENDON FC

Around 160 spectators, travelling in three coaches, came with us to Hendon Football Club. It was the first time that we had played on a proper football ground in front of a large crowd, so we were feeling both nervous and proud in equal measure. Our opponents in the final were the formidable Foden Ladies team from Sandbach in Cheshire. They were the team that had emerged as International Champions the previous year. With an average age of about twenty-four, they were a mature and experienced side. They had players who had been playing since the early 1960s for famous sides like Dick, Kerr Ladies (Sheila Parker) and Manchester Corinthians (Sylvia Gore) and were following in their footsteps as a northern works team that played unofficial matches to raise money for charity. We were definitely going into the match as the underdogs. The prize at stake was £100 and a place in the International Final at Belle Vue Stadium in Manchester.

In front of an intimidating crowd of 1,000–2,000, most of whom were supporting Foden Ladies, we were unfortunately both out-cheered and outplayed that day. Unable to match their team for strength and skill, we were trounced by six goals to nil. We were at a physical disadvantage as much as anything else, as we were essentially girls and they were women. It was like David against Goliath, except that we didn't have any other weapons at our disposal to make up for the strength difference!

They had a superb forward line that ran our defence ragged. As right-back, I had to cope with their extremely skilful and speedy left winger Lesley Cauldwell, while my colleagues had Sylvia Gore (who would go on to become the first ever goal-scorer for England) coming at them from the inside right position. It was not a comfortable experience! Sheila Parker (who was to go on to captain the first official England team) was formidable in the heart of their defence and our forwards, who had been so prolific in previous rounds of the competition, were unable to penetrate. Even though Foden's were reduced to ten players when their outside right, Sue Fish, was sent off for kicking one of our players, it made little difference to the outcome. Incidentally this was an

HENDON FOOTBALL CLUB
CLAREMONT ROAD   CRICKLEWOOD   LONDON, N.W.2

HUGHIE GREEN

in Association with

HOLIDAY CAMPS

PRESENTS

ALL ENGLAND FINAL

of

LADIES TELEVISION FOOTBALL LEAGUE

FODEN LADIES
CHESHIRE

v

THAME LADIES
OXFORDSHIRE

SUNDAY, 20th SEPTEMBER, 1970

KICK-OFF 3.00 p.m.

THANK YOU FOR YOUR SUPPORT

Right: Getting to the final of the Butlin's Cup with Thame, *c.* 1970.

Below: The team line-ups for the Butlin's Cup final, 20/9/70.

FODEN LADIES		
Colours:—Shirts —Sky Blue with Navy Stripes		
Shorts —Sky Blue		
Stockings —Sky Blue and Navy		

TEAM:—

Goalkeeper
WENDY HIGGINS

Right Back		Left Back
SHEILA PARKER (Capt.)		KATH STEENSON

Right Half	Centre Half	Left Half
PAULINE TAYLOR	YVONNE COOPER	ANN LATHAM

Inside Right		Inside Left
SYLVIA GORE		JOAN TENCH

Outside Right	Centre Forward	Outside Left
SUSAN FISH	GILLIAN CORNES	LESLEY CAULDWELL

Substitutes:—ELAINE BROWN   **Referee:**—MR. K. FRANKLIN
JOANNE WOLDRIDGE   Middlesex

How They Reached the Final:

Round One	Foden Ladies 2 — The Blue Diamonds 0
Round Two	Foden Ladies 6 — Kingston Ladies 0
Round Three	Foden Ladies 4 — Old Bank Ladies 0
Zone Final	Foden Ladies 5 — Fleece Fillies 0
Inter-Zone Final	Foden Ladies 2 — Ulcerby Sapphires 0

GOALS FOR 19, AGAINST NIL

THAME LADIES		
Colours:—Shirts — White		
Shorts — Red		
Stockings — Red		

TEAM:—

Goalkeeper
S. WALKER

Right Back		Left Back
W. OWEN		SHEILA FRENCH

Right Half	Centre Half	Left Half
M. DAWSON	SANDRA FRENCH	S. GOODWIN (Capt.)

Inside Right		Inside Left
J. HOPKINS		B. CASWELL

Outside Right	Centre Forward	Outside Left
M. McGROATY	A. EAST	Y. BLAINE

Linesmen:—MR. C. LIFFORD Middlesex   **Substitutes:**—S. ENTWISTLE
MR. J. FAWNING Middlesex   A. GLOVER

How They Reached the Final:

Round One	Bye
Round Two	Walkover
Round Three	Thame Ladies 9 — Legs United 0
Round Four	Thame Ladies 3 — Clacton Ladies 2
Zone Final	Thame Ladies 3 — Woolpit Bluebirds 1
Inter-Zone Finals	Thame Ladies 9 — Niton Dollies 0

GOALS FOR 24, AGAINST 3

historic event, which made the newspapers, as she was the first woman ever to be reported to the FA.

All in all Foden's gave us a football lesson. They were more organised, more balanced as a team and far more tactically aware. We had got away with it up until then as we hadn't come up against any tough opposition. Although it felt awful at the time and we travelled home both shell-shocked and thoroughly dejected, in the long run, losing that match in that way was the best thing that could have happened to us. While Foden's went on to beat Westhorn United from Scotland in the International final in Manchester, we went away to lick our wounds and plan our revenge. We discussed the game together, in detail, identified our weaknesses and what we needed to do about them and set ourselves an important goal: to challenge Foden Ladies to a return match as soon as possible and this time to beat them!

GRAND CHALLENGE MATCH: THAME LADIES *v.* FODEN LADIES, 27 JUNE 1971, NEGRETTI AND ZAMBIA'S SPORTS GROUND, STOCKDALE, AYLESBURY

The following season was spent in working towards this important objective. We were a club on a mission. Under the guidance of Micky Way (from Oxford United) and Mick Stockwell (who played for a local team) we trained harder to get physically stronger and fitter. We also worked on team tactics and got ourselves more organised to cope with set plays, like corners and free-kicks (when we had lost to Foden's we hadn't even built a defensive wall against their free-kicks).

The fruits of our labour began to show in our performance in the Oxfordshire League. By the end of the 1970/71 season, we had won the league and the league combination trophy and come runners-up in the President's Cup. We all agreed that the time was right to challenge Foden Ladies to that rematch.

As the Butlin's Cup did not take place in the summer of 1971 (it was, in fact, never held again due to the fact that the WFA had fallen out with the organisers and sponsors, who thereafter ceased their involvement in women's football[1]) we decided to challenge Foden's to play us in a friendly match in aid of charity. They duly accepted and the game was scheduled to take place on Sunday 27 June 1971; less than a year since our previous encounter.

The Oxford United directors were approached and asked if they would send one of their players to kick off the match and present the plaques at the end. Ron Atkinson ('Big Ron') was the Oxford United captain at the time and he agreed to come and do the honours. As a result of excellent publicity throughout the Aylesbury area, 600 spectators turned up to watch the spectacle. This was a fantastic crowd for a friendly women's football match at that time.

Our team for the match had been completely reshaped and bore little resemblance to the team that had been beaten so soundly the previous September. Our goalkeeper, Sally Walker, retained her place – she was a courageous player who thought nothing of diving at the feet of advancing attackers – but the rest of the defence had undergone a major overhaul. As the only remaining member of the original back three, I had been moved from right full-back into the centre. This was a position that I was to make my own in the coming years, for both my club and country. Lynda Harris filled my place at right-back. Our centre forward from the previous game (Ali East) had been moved to left-back and a new player, Tina Oliver (signed from Luton Daytels) had replaced her up front. This proved to be an inspired bit of team selection. Ali turned out to be an excellent left-back, who played in that position for quite a few years to come, while Tina Oliver scored four of the goals that we put past Foden Ladies in our thrilling 5-3 victory on that day. Bernie Caswell scored our fifth with a tap-in, while Sylvia Gore, Lesley Cauldwell and Anne Latham netted for Foden's. Shirley Entwhistle came in as left wing for us. An intelligent player and an excellent dead-ball kicker, she was given the task of taking most of our corners.

Other new faces in our team were Carol Bowerman, a tall, strong midfielder, and Gillian Sayell, who came in at outside right. At just fourteen years of age Gill was the youngest player on the pitch (there was no under-sixteen or under-nineteen football in those days, it was all open age) but as the local newspaper report of the match confirmed, she 'caused the Foden defence trouble with her speedy runs and dribbling down the wing.' A remarkable young talent, Gill was invited to join an unofficial England squad that went out to Mexico that year (1971) to play in an unofficial Women's World Cup competition. She was not able to play for us for a while on her return, as she received a ban from the WFA, for being a part of an unsanctioned England team. Going to Mexico was a fantastic, once-in-a-lifetime experience, however (the matches were played in front of thousands of fanatical supporters, with the final staged in the Aztec Stadium), so I am sure that she felt that it was worth it.

Turning a 6-0 defeat into a 5-3 victory, against one of the strongest teams in women's football at the time, was a big achievement for us as a club. This time it was Foden's turn to be shell-shocked, as I am sure that they came expecting to win again. Less than a year on, however, we were a team with more expertise and maturity than the one that had been humbled at Hendon. We also had an excellent team spirit. Totally focused and psyched up for the game, our approach was very much 'all for one and one for all' and it paid off.

Ron Atkinson had stayed to watch the whole match and presented both teams and the officials with commemorative plaques and medals at the end. Bernard Caswell, who was influential in setting up the match (in aid of children with learning difficulties), had looked after 'Big Ron' during the game and chatted to him on the sideline. At one point during the game Bernard had gone to find them both a cup of tea. While he was away, his daughter, Bernie Caswell, who was a tough, uncompromising midfield player in our team (she was as solid as a brick wall and took no prisoners!) had an altercation with Sylvia Gore from Foden's. Bernie lost her temper and swung around at her. When Bernard returned with the tea, Atkinson pointed at Bernie and said, 'Is that your daughter?' When Bernard confirmed that it was, he exclaimed, 'Well she's just had a go at that girl from Foden's!' Overall, Ron Atkinson was apparently very complimentary about the game. He had not been involved with women's football before and was impressed with the skill, tackling and general standard of the women players on show that day.

THE 1971/72 SEASON

Victory over Foden's in the summer of 1971 proved to be the catalyst that our club needed to send us on to bigger and better things during the following season. We had outgrown the Oxfordshire League and entered the recently formed and more challenging Home Counties League, as we needed better competition if we were to continue to improve. This league was affiliated to the WFA and was a product of the rapid growth of women's football since the inception of the WFA in 1969 (there were forty-four affiliated clubs in 1969 and nearly 100 at the start of the 1971/72 season[2]).

Although we were good enough to go straight into the First Division, we had to start in the Second Division and earn our spurs. The Home Counties League Cup did, however, bring us up against First Division sides.

We were also entered into the WFA Mitre Cup. This was a national cup competition that had been set up by the WFA (sponsored by Mitre Sports) during the previous (1970/71) season and was to become the most prestigious cup competition in women's football (the equivalent of the men's FA Cup).

Playing in these new competitions meant that we had to travel much further afield for our matches than previously. This broadened our horizons and brought us into contact with some of the top teams of the time, such as Southampton, Foden Ladies, Crystal Palace and Leicester EMGALS. It also proved to be more expensive, however. As far as financing the club was concerned, there was no lottery funding, or other grant aid available and sponsorship was, at this time, hard to come by. Consequently, whatever money we needed, we had to raise ourselves. Colin French recalls that it cost £600 to fund the team for the first three competitive seasons. Most of this came from players' subs, a weekly tote and a monthly disco. We also held a collection at matches, as we were well supported. The coach firm that we used in the early days gave us a reasonable deal, while later we became one of the few teams to own our own bus. This self-sufficient approach was fairly typical of how most women's teams operated at the time.

Being a member of Thame Ladies Football Club wasn't just about the football however. Although competing and winning was important to us, there was far more to it than that. We were a group of young girls who were looking for fun, friendship and new experiences. Being fairly close in age, we enjoyed each other's company off the field as well as on it.

Although some of the girls had boyfriends, when we got together (for what usually ended up as a weekend of entertainment, rather than just ninety minutes of football) it was definitely a girl thing! It was an opportunity for a bit of female bonding away from the inhibiting presence of men (apart from our male managers and trainer, who were quite good at keeping a watchful eye without spoiling our fun). We often got together on a Saturday at one of the local hostelries in Thame (either the Four Horseshoes or the Jolly Sailor), which we would turn into our own social club for the evening. We were serious about our football though and, as we played on a Sunday, we didn't imbibe too many lemonades on the night before the match!

Because we often had to leave early the next morning, the girls from outside the Thame area, Paddy McGroarty, Nancy Roy (who was another army girl and a close friend of Paddy's, who played in goal for us that season), Maureen Dawson and myself, would usually end up staying over at the home of the manager (Colin French) and his long-suffering wife (Geraldine French). They had five children of their own, but always seemed happy to throw their home open to the girls from the team. Their house, in Essex Road, became like a second home to me at weekends. We would often all stay together in one room and, according to Colin and Geraldine, I kept the other girls awake at night, telling jokes and stories!

Playing on a Sunday and the extensive travelling also caused problems with getting back at a reasonable time, especially as we had to stop at some watering holes on the way back for 'refreshments'! Fed up with waiting for her return, Bernie Caswell's parents used to go to bed and lock the front door. She became very adept at climbing in through a window. I had to be picked up from Thame and driven home to Beaconsfield, which was quite a long way, so I was even later to bed than everyone else. I then had to try to be alert at school the next day, during what was my 'A' Level year. Fortunately I had already secured a place at PE teacher training college for the forthcoming September, on the strength of my sporting profile and my 'O' Level results.

Although I was struggling to find the time to keep up with my studies, the football was going extremely well. As predicted, we were in reality too good to be in the Second Division of the Home Counties League and were winning matches easily. By the end of the season we emerged as Second Division

THAME Shirts RED Shorts WHITE		CRYSTAL PALACE Shirts CLARET & BLUE Shorts WHITE
N. Roy	1	S. Hazelton
L. Harris	2	M. Wilson
A. East	3	L. Lowe
M. Dawson	4	L. Penfold
W. Owen	5	J. Clarke
S. Entwistle	6	I. Lecorre
G. Sayell	7	H. Ross
J. Hopkins	8	D. Beauchamp
B. Caswell	9	S. Corderoy
S. French	10	B. Dolling
M. Mc. Groaty	11	K. Evans
S. Walker	12	A. Smith
G. Eele	13	S. Carson

REFEREE   J. Whicker
LINESMEN   T. Gammons
           A. N. Other

The LEAGUE CUP will be presented by Mr. B. Head, Manager of Crystal Palace F.C.

HOME COUNTIES WOMEN'S FOOTBALL LEAGUE. Est. 1970   1971/1972 Season

LEAGUE CUP FINAL

THAME

v

CRYSTAL PALACE

KICK OFF 3.00 p.m. APRIL 23rd 1972

BRACKNELL TOWN F.C.

The **Bracknell News**
For Sport

Above left: Runners-up in the Home Counties League Cup with Thame in our first season in the Home Counties League, *c. 1972.*

Above right: Team line-ups for the Home Counties League Cup final, 23/4/72.

champions, securing promotion to the First Division at the first attempt. We also appeared in three cup finals. We won the Vice-President's Cup and the Cystic Fibrosis Cup. Both of these competitions were organised by the Midlands League. In the Home Counties League Cup, which involved teams from both divisions of the Home Counties League we were beaten by First Division champions Crystal Palace in the final. Bertie Head, the Crystal Palace men's team manager had been invited to present the cup. He ended up handing it over to his own daughter, Sue Corderoy, who was captain of the Crystal Palace team!

THE WFA (MITRE) CUP

A fantastic season was really made special, however, by an excellent WFA (Mitre) Cup run. Eighty-six teams had entered this most prestigious of knock-out cup competitions (fifteen more than during the previous season, when the competition had been in its inaugural year[3]). These were arranged into eight regional groups, with the group winners progressing to the quarter-finals. We emerged as winners of our group and joined Lees Ladies (formerly Stewarton and Thistle), Foden Ladies, EMGALS (Leicester), Aston Villa, Deal Town, Crystal Palace 'A' and Southampton 'A' in the quarter finals.[4] By chance, we were drawn against the old enemy Foden Ladies once again!

WFA (MITRE) CUP QUARTER-FINAL: THAME LADIES v. FODEN LADIES, 1972

The match was played at Thame United FC, which gave us the home advantage. Foden's had to travel all the way down from Cheshire. A good crowd of several hundred people turned up to watch yet another exciting encounter between our two teams, which finished all square at full-time. The game went into extra time and this time our youthfulness versus their maturity was an asset rather than a disadvantage. They began to tire quite noticeably during the time added on (their long journey was probably a contributory factor) while our superior fitness and younger legs carried us through to victory. Our midfield strength was also crucial. We had strong, aggressive players like Bernie Caswell and Maureen (Mo) Dawson, who didn't flinch from tackles, and a fantastic playmaker in Paddy McGroarty, who was at the heart of things as usual. Shirley Entwhistle was also influential. Possessing one of the hardest kicks in women's football at that time, she came on in extra time to convert a penalty with a shot that nearly burst their net!

WFA MITRE CUP SEMI-FINAL: THAME LADIES v. SOUTHAMPTON, 1972

Having beaten Foden's, we met Southampton in the semi-finals. This was a very tough draw indeed, as they had won the competition the previous year and were about to emerge as the major force in women's football for that era (during the period 1971-1981 Southampton won the WFA Cup eight times). They had some excellent players, five of whom went on to play for England, and a lot of experience: they had won the prestigious Deal International Tournament in 1970 and, after winning the inaugural WFA Mitre Cup trophy in 1971, had toured the USA, playing exhibition matches against Roma Ladies, who were a top Italian side.[5]

Despite Southampton's impressive credentials, we gave them a good run for their money. The semi-final was an extremely close affair, which we lost narrowly by three goals to four, with our centre forward, Jayne Hopkins, scoring a hat-trick. Southampton actually complimented us on our play that day. I think that they were pleased to have had a bit of competition for a change, as they had been winning all their matches far too easily.

Clubs That Entered for the Womens Football Association Mitre Challenge Trophy 1971—72

Group 1
Westthorn United LFC
Prima Donnas
Fife Dynamites
2 * Stewarton Thistle LFC (now Lees Ladies) ← *Ladies Finalists*
Dundee Strikers LFC
Hooverettes

Group 2
Manchester Nomads
Macclesfield LFC
Southport Supporters
Howards Awardians
* Fodens
Reckitts Ladies
Forest LFC
Manchester Corinthian
Belle Vue Belles
Plessey LFC
Preston North End Supporters Club
Blackpool Supporters LFC

Group 3
Nuneaton Rangers LFC
Bedworth Rangers LFC
Rainbow Dazzlers WFC
Western Athletic
3 * Emgals Ladies FC
Hillmorton Hunters LFC
Lansdowne LFC
Leicester City Supporters Club LFC
Coventry Bantam LFC
Bedworth LFC
Rye Piece LFC
Wanderers LFC (Nuneaton)
Renold LFC

Group 4
* Aston Villa LFC
Dudley Road Hospital LFC
Norton Ladies
Kays LFC
Robirch
Villa Rangers LFC
Droitwich St. Andrews LFC
Lodge Park LFC
Lan-Bar Ladies
Badsey LFC
Swan Rangers LFC

Group 5
Lydd Ladies
Barnfield LFC
Ladybirds LFC (Herne Bay)
Margate Rangers LFC
Deal Town LFC
Maidstone Mote United
Ramsgate All Stars LFC
Thanet United LFC
Medway Ladies
Crusaders LFC
Folkestone United
White Wanderers (Hamstreet)

Group 6
Willie Walker Wonders
Bosom Buddies United LFC
Arland Ladies FC
Luton Ladies
Farley United (Tigers)
L'Oreal Ladies FC
4 * Thame Girls
Boreham Wood Hearts Ladies
Beechfield Ladies
Blue Birds (Woolpit) LFC
Barking Belles

Group 7
Crystal Palace Ladies 'B'
Courthope Ladies
Hellingly Hospital S. & S. Club
Bluebirds LFC
Spurs LFC
Fulham
Brighton GPO LFC
Queens Park Rangers
* Crystal Palace Ladies 'A'
White Ribbon
Aristocats Utd
Orient LFC

Group 8
1 * Southampton 'A'
Swindon Spitfires
Newbury Golden Eagles
Bracknell Bullitts
Southampton 'B'
Johnson Rangers
Reading Ladies
Devizes Moonrakers LFC
Farmborough LFC

WFA Cup, 1971/72 season.
List of teams taking part in the competition.

WFA (MITRE CUP) THIRD AND FOURTH POSITION PLAY-OFF, BURTON ALBION FC, MAY 1972

Losing in the semi-final stages was a blow, but we still went on to participate in the excitement of cup final day. As a curtain raiser to the main event, we were involved in a third and fourth place play-off match against the other losing semi-finalists, EMGALS Ladies from Leicester. The match took place at Burton Albion FC in Burton-on-Trent. There was a good crowd in attendance; about 1,500 watched Southampton beat Lees Ladies from Scotland in the final at 3.45 p.m. and many of these had turned up early to watch our game, which kicked off at 2 p.m. Our match was a very exciting and close contest but, unfortunately, we ended up on the losing side of things and finished in fourth place.

Although our final placing in the Mitre Cup was a bit of a disappointment to us at the time, coming fourth out of eighty-six teams drawn from all over

The W.F.A. Mitre Challenge Trophy

FINALS

to be played on 7th May 1972
at the ground of Burton Albion F.C., Eton Park, Burton-on-Trent

Losing Semi-Finalists Final

Start	Half-Time	Finish
2.00 p.m.	2.40 p.m. to 2.45 p.m.	3.25 p.m.

(If a draw at full time)   No extra time, penalties to decide the winners

GRAND FINAL

3.45 p.m.	4.25 p.m. to 4.30 p.m.	5.10 p.m.

Extra time will be played if a draw at full-time. Then penalties to decide the winners if still a draw.

Teams and Officals of the Losing Semi-Finalists Final

Thame Ladies (Oxford)	*Emgals (Leicester)*
1. Nancy Roy	1. Lynda Shave
2. Alison East	2. Angela Miles
3. Lynn Harris	3. Joy Ashby
4. Maureen Dawson	4. Jane Noble
5. Wendy Owen	5. June Foulke
6. Shirley Entwistle	6. Christine Poole
7. Gillian Sayell	7. Jackie Freakley
8. Jane Hopkins	8. Joan Briggs
9. Sandra French	9. Jill Stockley
10. Bernadette Coswell	10. Marion Crook
11. Margaret McGroarty	11. Sally Clay
12. Sally Walker	12. Betty Mitchell
13. Gloria Eele	13. Gladys Nielson
14. Carol Mead	14. Karen Malpas

Referee: Mr. A. P. J. Gwynne (Leamington Spa)	*Linesmen:* Mr. F. Sivom (Walsall) Mr. T. Sheppard (Leamington Spa)

Teams and Officals of the Grand Final

Lees Ladies Formerly (Stewarton and Thistle) (Scotland)	*Southampton*
1. Gerry Chalmers	1. Sue Buckett
2. Betty Brogan	2. Karen Buchanan
3. Mary-Jane Lindsay	3. Pauline Dickie
4. Linda Kidd	4. Jill Osman
5. Jean Hunter	5. Jill Long
6. Sandra Walker	6. Maureen Case
7. Rose Riley	7. Lynda Hale
8. Jan Lightbody	8. Lesley Lloyd
9. Susie Ferries	9. Pat Judd
10. Margaret McCunnis	10. Sue Lopez
11. Mary White	11. Pat Davies
Subs: Sophia McDonald Isabel Howie	Subs: Sue Stubbs Shirley O'Callaghan

Referee: Mr. W. Tidman (Bedworth)	*Linesmen:* Mr. D. Dowie (Leicester) Mr. J. O. Jones (Overseal)

4

WFA Cup, 1971/72 season. Team lists for the final (Southampton v. Lees Ladies) and third and fourth place play-off (Thame v. EMGALS).

England and Scotland was, in hindsight, a fantastic result for a young team that was in only its third season of competition. Our successful run in the competition also inadvertently helped us to improve the club's facilities, which had been rudimentary to say the least.

We played on the local football pitch in Thame, but there were no changing rooms. This was particularly problematic for the visiting teams, some of who had long journeys to make after the game. In an effort to improve the situation, we enlisted the help of the local newspaper, who willingly took up our cause. At one home game, in the Mitre Cup, the weather and the pitch were particularly atrocious. We all got absolutely saturated and caked in mud from head to foot. When we came off the field at the end of the game, you couldn't even make out the original colours of our playing kit. Both teams were in such a state that drastic measures were called for to get us cleaned up. The local paper the following week carried our match report, which highlighted the dressing-room problem, and told readers that after the match 'the ladies had to be led down to the town cattle market, like a herd of cows, to be hosed down!' This was exactly what had taken place. We soon discovered the power of the press. After this appeared in the paper, the embarrassed local council responded immediately and money was found to fund changing rooms at the Thame football pitch, complete with full toilet and shower facilities.

If there was a dearth of proper changing facilities in women's football in the 1970s, then gaining access to qualified medical support was no less of a problem. It was not until I played for England that I enjoyed the services of a team physiotherapist. In the modern women's game, FA-affiliated clubs are supposed to ensure that a qualified first aider is available at every match. To be classed as a good club and be kite-marked with the FA's Charter Standard, someone also has to have attended an FA treatment of injuries course.

Things were very different to this playing club football for Thame. Basically it was still the era of the good old bucket and sponge. The bucket was ready on the touchline, filled with cold water, and anyone might be chosen to run on with it when someone went to ground, writhing in agony. It was a cure for all ills and a good way of stopping players from feigning injury (they could usefully bring it back into the men's Premiership!). If you didn't fancy a cold soaking, then it was advisable to jump up quickly when you saw the bucket on its way.

For post-match bruises, there were always the trusty animal liniments. Geraldine French's father was a cattle dealer and at the house in Essex Road they kept a box of green oils for the treatment of such injuries. On one occasion when I was staying over, I was given the job of applying 'the green stuff' to Sandra French's swollen ankle. As I was rubbing it in, I began to read out the instructions on the label. It said, 'For cows' udders, teats and all sorts of sores. Massage and rub in well.' For some reason, on hearing this information, Sandra burst into tears!

FRANCE TRIP: MAY 1972

In May 1972, just before I was due to sit my 'A' Level exams, Thame Ladies embarked on a long-weekend trip to France, to play football against a club side from near the city of Chartres. Women's football was also taking off in Europe at this time and this was to be our first foray against overseas opposition.

As we had to pay for the trip ourselves, it had to be a fairly low-budget affair. We flew from Lydd Airport in Kent on a tiny thirty-seater plane, which we shared with a boys' football team that was also going 'on tour' to France. Although a bit nerve-racking, due to the size of the plane, the outward flight was pretty uneventful.

My problems began when we arrived at our final destination and I realised that somewhere along the way I had managed to lose my passport! The other girls in the team seemed to think that this was hilarious and proceeded to tease me mercilessly about it for the entire weekend. They managed to convince me that I wouldn't be allowed to return home with them at the end of the trip, but would have to remain at the British Embassy in Paris, until a new passport could be arranged for me. I think that I must have been very gullible in my youth, because I fell for this story hook, line and sinker. I spent most of the time in France worrying that I would be detained and miss my forthcoming 'A' Level exams.

The weekend was also rather tense because instead of being accommodated together as a team, we were split up and farmed out to French families. I stayed with a young couple in their town apartment. They were very hospitable and keen to introduce me to their relatives. On the day of the football match against the French side, I was invited to a five-course Sunday lunch at the home of one their parents. I had to wade through all this food only an hour before the kick-off. I couldn't refuse any of it as they had gone to so much trouble and were so determined that I should enjoy it. When I joined up with the rest of the girls to play the game, I discovered that everyone else had had a similar experience. Sandra French, who was at that point playing alongside me in the middle of a back four, was probably the most nauseous among us during that match. She had complimented her family on the beautiful steak that they had given her for dinner, only to be informed that what she had in fact eaten was horsemeat!

Despite the unintended attempts to sabotage our performance, we won the match comfortably and rounded off a successful stay with a sightseeing trip to the cathedral city of Chartres. When the coach returned to pick us up on the Monday to take us back to the airport, I was highly relieved to be reunited with my passport. I was not going to be detained in France and miss my exams after all. Luckily we had the same coach driver, who had discovered it under a seat and held on to it for me. It wasn't until this point that my colleagues (who were supposed to be my friends) informed me that I would most probably have been allowed home without my passport anyway.

Losing my passport had been traumatic enough, but the worst nightmare of the trip was still to come. It probably marked the start of my lifelong fear of flying. We were travelling back in a small plane again, but this time it was far from uneventful. When we came in to land at Lydd Airport, it became apparent that the pilot was not in full control of proceedings. First of all he narrowly missed landing in a nearby field instead of on the airport runway. Then he put the plane down on two wheels, at a sideways angle and came abruptly to a halt, narrowly missing the airport building! Following this terrifying experience, whenever I had to travel by air with the England squad the team doctor, Ernie Taylor, had to prescribe valium for me. They would never have managed to get me on the plane without it.

DEAL INTERNATIONAL TOURNAMENT: JULY 1972

Coming fourth in the Mitre Cup in May 1972 gained us entry into the prestigious Deal International Tournament. Arthur Hobbs, from Deal in Kent, who was dedicated to the development of women's football, started the tournament in 1967. As a result of its great success, he went on to found the WFA (in 1969) to govern the sport and was the organisation's first secretary. He was also instrumental in lobbying the FA to lift the 1921 ban.[6] All the top clubs that had done well in the WFA (Mitre) Cup and their league went into the Deal International Tournament, plus teams invited from Europe and Scotland, to give it an international flavour. Previous illustrious winners had included Manchester Corinthians, Southampton and Stewarton & Thistle.[7]

We felt proud and excited at the prospect of being invited to take part. The event was a weekend affair, which took place in the summer in a coastal town, so we were also looking forward to some fun in the sun! We travelled down on the Friday night and were accommodated in small groups at bed and breakfast guesthouses in the town. Games (approximately fifteen minutes each way) were held on the Saturday and Sunday and drew good crowds of spectators. Saturday night was a chance for the girls from all the different teams to get together to socialise, talk football and enjoy a few drinks (in moderation of course!) before the serious business recommenced the next day. Friendships were made across international boundaries and notes were compared about how women's football was progressing in the different countries. For some reason I can remember the social side of the tournament more clearly than the football!

While I cannot recall many of the finer details of the football action, I do know what the outcome was. We won the tournament at our first attempt to become the last team to win this historic tournament. 1972 was to be the final year that the tournament was staged, probably due to the fact that the WFA Cup was now in place and Arthur Hobbs was scaling down his involvement in women's football. He retired as secretary of the WFA in 1972 and sadly died a few years later.

All in all, the 1971/72 season had proved to be an extremely busy and tremendously successful one for Thame Ladies. It was one in which we played excellent football, really worked hard and pulled together as a team. By the end of it we had collected a significant haul of silverware for our trophy cabinet and were becoming local celebrities. The *Thame Gazette* carried a story about our meteoric rise to fame, which was accompanied by a photograph of the squad, surrounded by various cups and trophies.

None of these achievements would have been possible, however, without the work of a number of dedicated volunteers, which was fairly typical of how the sport of women's football managed to develop in this era. These included our team managers Colin French and Don Merrilees; our trainers Mick Stockwell and Micky Way; Gill Sayell's mum and dad, Bob and Popsy, who did a lot of organising; Geraldine French, an unsung heroine, who housed and fed half the team every weekend and Harold Dawson (Maureen Dawson's father), a regular supporter, who came to most away matches and mended the bus when it broke down. At the time, I am sure that the players took all this for granted. In hindsight it is true to say that, without the hard work and dedication of this small group of people, we would never have had the opportunity to play women's football, let alone to do it so successfully.

It had been a long season, one in which we had played an awful lot of football, but for some of us it wasn't over yet. We still had the trials for the first ever official England women's team to look forward to!

ENGLAND TRIALS: SUMMER 1972

Although I obviously must have possessed some worthy footballing attributes (according to Bernard Caswell I had a good kick, was strong in the tackle and fearless when it came to heading the ball, irrespective of whether or not I got hit in the process), when I look back at how I came to be selected to play for England, I always feel that there was a strong element of luck involved. On several counts I was in the right place at the right time. Firstly, I was fortunate to have been picked up by Thame Ladies and to have become involved in their successes in high-profile cup competitions and a WFA-affiliated league. This allowed my skills to develop, flourish and, most importantly, to be recognised. Secondly, I was lucky that I was playing football at a critical transition point in the history of women's football, a time when the sport was becoming more officially organised and structured and the FA had been persuaded to lift its stifling restrictions and offer some measure of recognition and support to the game.

These factors all came together in the summer of 1972. The WFA decided that the time was right in the development of the women's game to organise trials for the first official England women's team. Recognition by the FA, in February 1972, led to them agreeing to appoint and pay the expenses of the England team manager; all other aspects of the running of the England team were to be left to the WFA, who set-up an international-team committee to oversee matters.[8]

Trials were organised in a two-phase structure. Firstly there was an inter-league trial tournament involving league representative teams from the various leagues up and down the country that were affiliated to the WFA. Approximately 300 players were involved in this.[9] From this tournament, twenty-five players were to be selected by the England manager to go forward to final trials in the September. Four players from Thame Ladies (Paddy McGroarty, Sandra French, Gill Sayell and I) had been picked to play for the

Home Counties League representative team as a result of trials that had occurred previously, so we were automatically involved in this England team selection process. Our league side was very strong (it contained a large contingent from the Southampton team) and we ended up winning the England inter-league competition. This was another factor that I believe helped to bring me to the attention of the England manager.

Of the Thame players in the Home Counties team, both myself and Paddy McGroarty were called up for the final England trials weekend, which was to be held at Loughborough College (now Loughborough University) from 15–17 September 1972. This was just before I was due to go to Dartford College to start my physical education teacher training course. When I heard that I had been selected to go further, I really had to pinch myself. It was a really exciting time as I now had both my lifelong ambitions within my sights.

ENGLAND FINAL TRIALS WEEKEND: LOUGHBOROUGH COLLEGE,
15-17 SEPTEMBER 1972

Eric Worthington had been appointed as the first England manager. As an FA staff coach, a senior lecturer at Loughborough and an ex-Queens Park Rangers and Watford player, he had excellent credentials for the job. Because of his Loughborough connections we were fortunate to be able to stay for the weekend

Programme for the England national trial match for selecting the first ever England squad, held at Leicester City's training ground, c. 1972.

W. F. A.
ENGLAND
TRIAL

PROBABLES
vs
POSSIBLES

17th Sept. 1972

The Players...

JEANNIE ALLOTT (16) Has been playing football for 8 years for Fodens. Comes from Crewe.

JANET BAGGULEY (17) Born in Buxton and plays for Macclesfield. Also plays netball.

JO BOWMAN (17) Plays for Preston North End F.C., and is a Cub Scout Leader.

KATARINA BOZIC (22) Is a nurse, and plays for Birmingham City. Also enjoys basketball.

SUE BUCKETT (28) A member of the successful team from Southampton. Goalkeeper.

SANDRA CHOAT (15) Lives in Woking and has recently joined Amersham Angels L.F.C.

PAT DAVIES (17) Another member of Southampton team, and she also likes hockey & tennis.

EILEEN FOREMAN (18) Played football for 1 year. Born at Frome but now lives in Warminster.

JACKIE FULLER (17) A machinist from Alvaston who plays for Hectors Edition. Supports Man. Utd.

SYLVIA GORE (27) Another member of Fodens & has played football for 14 years.

SANDRA GRAHAM (27) Born in Warrington but now lives & plays in Blackpool. Likes crosswords.

RAYNER HADDEN (17) Comes from Redditch & plays for Lan-bar Ladies. Is a skittles expert.

LYNDA HALE (18) Yet another Southamptonian who has been playing for 6 years.

JACKIE HUGHES (20) Lives in Bootle and has played for Liverton for 2 years.

MORAG KIRKLAND (15) The fourth girl from Southampton, who also plays volleyball and tennis.

JULIA MANNING (20) Plays for Lowestoft & supports Norwich City. Enjoys horse-riding.

PADDY McGROARTY (24) A member of Thame L.F.C. and one of England's cleverest ball-players.

MARGARET MIKS (16) Lives and plays in Coventry, and is a County athlete and hockey player.

PAULINE MORRIS (23) Plays football for L'Oreal L.F.C. from Leighton Buzzard.

WENDY OWEN (18) The second Thames L.F.C. player and a keen pot-holer. Plays the guitar.

SHEILA PARKER (24) Housewife and third member of Fodens L.F.C. Has a 9-month-old boy.

LESLEY STIRLING (15) A lassie from Lancashire who plays for Preston North End Ladies F.C.

SUSAN WHYATT (16) Comes from Macclesfield and has been playing football for 2 years.

JEAN WILSON (23) A bank clerk from Manchester who plays for Manchester Corinthians.

JOAN BRIGGS (30) A Leicester Emgal who has been helping England Manager, Eric Worthington.

The twenty-five final trialists for the very first England squad.

at what was (and still is) one of the top colleges for physical education and sport in England. The twenty-five players who arrived at the college on the Friday evening were drawn from all around the country and ranged in age from fifteen to thirty. We were a motley crew including schoolgirls, bank clerks, office workers, two housewives and a nurse. We had access to the college's sports and lecture room facilities and stayed in the student halls of residence. As well as the England manager, three officials from the WFA International Team Committee were in attendance to deal with any problems, Gladys Aikin, Pat Gregory and Roger Ebben. This whole set-up made me feel very valued and part of something that was far more organised and professional than anything that I had experienced previously in my involvement in women's football. I was desperate to perform well over the weekend and make the cut to the final fifteen.

The programme included coaching and training sessions (both practical and theoretical) and culminated in a 'Probables' v. 'Possibles' match, which was held at Leicester City's training ground in Aylestone, at 3 p.m. on the Sunday afternoon. We had a full day of educational sessions on the Saturday (which started at 9.15 in the morning and ended at 9 in the evening) and a half-day on Sunday, before being given some free time to relax and prepare for the match. Eric Worthington, who was entirely responsible for the delivery of the sessions, covered some technical, strategic and fitness topics that he obviously felt were going to be fundamental to the success of a future England team. These included passing practices, principles of play, attacking in the front third, attacking and defending at set plays and fitness training methods.

The England trials weekend was a great learning experience but it was also very nerve-racking as we knew that at the end of it ten of us would be discarded. Everyone was determined not to be one of them, so play was very competitive with players trying hard to impress the England manager, even before the actual trial match. As the weekend progressed, you got an idea of who was in the frame to be picked for the squad by the line-up that the manager was using in sessions on set plays. I got the sense that I was not central to his thinking. This was confirmed when the teams were announced for Sunday's match. I was selected to play for the 'Possibles', whereas all the top players from Foden Ladies and Southampton, plus my Thame teammate Paddy McGroarty, were playing against me on the 'Probables' side. Apart from anything else this was going to be a very hard game for my team and, as one of the two central defenders, I knew that it was going to be difficult to shine.

Everything about the match was conducted very professionally. We travelled to Leicester City's training ground to play a full ninety-minute match, officiated by a qualified referee and linesmen. The teams had proper strips to wear and separate dressing rooms. Eric Worthington visited each team, both before the game and at half-time, to give us a team talk.

As I feared, my team were overwhelmed by the opposition. By half-time the 'Possibles' were 5-1 down. We did slightly better in the second half but, with a final score of 7-1, I thought that as one of the hapless defenders on the losing side, my chances of being selected for the final England squad must now be pretty remote.

After the game we returned to Loughborough College for a meal and a closing talk by the England manager. He was not, however, going to announce his final squad that day. Instead we were sent away to face an agonising wait to receive the verdict by post! Reflecting on the weekend afterwards, I decided that it had been fantastic, as up to that point I had not really received any formal coaching in football. I had certainly never come into contact with such a highly qualified FA coach as Eric Worthington. Whereas today there are FA Coaching Centres and Centres of Excellence to nurture talented young female players at under-twelve, under-fourteen and under-sixteen level, none of this was in place at the time. The WFA was a voluntary organisation, operating on a shoestring budget, which at that time was mainly gleaned from affiliation fees and a small grant from the Sports Council. It didn't have the means to fund such a programme.

It wasn't until the Loughborough weekend that I realised how little I actually knew about the art of defending! The England manager had introduced us to the concept of patience and not diving into the tackle too soon, and demonstrated the art of jockeying and channelling the attacker, before putting in a well-timed challenge. I lapped all this information up and was determined to go away and put these new skills into practice, even if I was not chosen for the final England squad.

Incidentally, I did try to do this in my next few matches for Thame, but my club manager did not seem to be enamoured with my new *modus operandi*. He kept shouting at me from the sidelines to 'get stuck into the tackle' and became very exasperated at me for backing off and delaying the challenge. This went on for several weeks until finally I had had enough. Things came to a head when we were playing away at Stowmarket against the Woolpit Bluebirds. I was playing at right-back and our manager had been on my case from the outset. He kept following me up and down the touchline urging me to go straight in to try to dispossess their left winger. Bearing in mind what Eric Worthington had told me, I decided that this was not going to be the best tactic, as she had excellent close control and some nifty tricks up her sleeve, which would have left me flat on my backside, looking foolish. I therefore ignored him and stuck to my own game plan. Undeterred, he bravely stuck to his guns and continued to heckle. Suddenly, something inside me just snapped and the red mist descended. I marched off the pitch and over to my startled manager, removed my shorts and handed them to him. I can't remember my exact words to him but they were something along these lines: 'If you are so sure that you can do a better job than me, then you can go on and do it!' With this I marched off to the dressing room and locked myself in. It took the best efforts of both the manager's wife (Geraldine French) and our trainer (Mick Stockwell) to calm me down and talk me back out on to the field of play!

After the England trials weekend, I fortunately had little time to dwell on my negative thoughts about what the outcome might be. These were pushed to the back of my mind, as my head was full of the excitement of going away from home for the first time. I was due to start my three-year college course the very next week and there was all the preparation and packing still to do!

ENGLAND SELECTION: SEPTEMBER 1972

Shortly after I arrived at Dartford College (one of the premier women's physical education colleges at that time) to begin my teacher training, I received the all-important letter from the WFA; I had been selected for the England squad for the first official international match away to Scotland that coming November. I telephoned my parents straight away with the news and they were both proud and delighted for me. Needless to say, I was absolutely over the moon, especially as I had more or less convinced myself that I hadn't got through. The only problem was that I would need several days' leave from college to enable me to join up with the England party. Getting this permission proved to be no simple matter.

Women's PE colleges in the early 1970s were still like glorified girls' boarding schools. The regime was a fairly strict one, down to times by which the entrance doors to halls of residence were locked in the evenings. Woe betide anyone found in the wrong hall (or worse still with a man in the halls) after hours! This would earn you a dressing down from the principal and possible expulsion from your residence. There was a pastoral system in place, based on a 'family' structure. Incoming freshers were allocated a second year who acted as their 'college mother'. Their role was to help and mentor their 'daughter' on arrival and through the settling-in period. Your college mother's mother, in the third year, was your college grandmother! This might seem like a rather quaint and old-fashioned idea now, but it was in fact a very useful system that provided an important safety net for a young woman finding herself living away from home for the very first time.

I sought help from my college 'family' on how to get time off to represent my country. I was told that I would need to request an audience with the Principal, to ask her for official leave of absence. This would involve going to her house on campus at a specified time to plead my case. I was strongly advised by my peers that if I failed to wear a skirt for this mission then I could forget it, my request was sure to be denied!

THE WOMEN'S FOOTBALL ASSOCIATION

(INAUGURATED 1st NOVEMBER 1969)
(CAXTON HALL, LONDON)

OFFICERS   *Chairman*   Mr. D. Marlowe
     Vice Chairman   Mr. P. Guynne
     Treasurer   Mr. D. Hunt
     Asst. Sec.   Miss S. Lopez
     Registration Sec.   Mrs. G. Aiken

HON. SECRETARY   Miss P. Gregory

20/9/72

Dear *Wendy*

     I am pleased to confirm your selection by Mr. Eric Worthington, for his first England team of 15 players.

     As you will undoubtedly be interested in the complete team, Mr. Worthington has selected the following players;

Susan Buckett	Morag Kirkland	Sheila Parker(Captain)
Sandra Graham	Janet Bagguley	Paddy McGroaty
Lynda Hale	Sylvia Gore	Pat Davies
Jeannie Allott	Jean Wilson	Sue Wyatt
Wendy Owen	Eileen Foreman	Julia Manning.

     The 12 players underlined will compose the two 5-a-side teams to play at Wembley.

     Mr. Worthington intends to draft an information sheet, covering all the work you took part in during the Loughborough week-end, and as soon as I receive this I will send you a copy.

     You will receive information regarding matches and further training as soon as this is available.

     On behalf of the W.F.A., and of the International Committee I would like to offer our sincere congratulations on your success in reaching the goal of being an England Team Player.

Yours sincerely,

G. Aikin

G. Aikin(Mrs)
Chairman of the International Committee W.F.A.

Finding out that I had been selected for the very first England women's football squad!

And so it was that, several days later, I found myself, with great trepidation, ringing the principal's doorbell, feeling very uncomfortable in a skirt that I had borrowed from my college 'grandmother'. Our principal was a fairly small, greying, middle-aged married woman, who was approaching retirement. She was a strict disciplinarian of the 'old school' and as a new first-year student I was terrified at the prospect of having to go to see her so early in my college career. She answered the doorbell and ushered me into her study, where I blurted out the reason for my visit. The principal's response was not what I had expected and made me so mad that I had to struggle to stay outwardly calm. When I said that I wanted time off college to play football for England, she visibly blanched and said, 'Surely women playing football is just a joke?' As you can imagine I was not amused. I had played and trained hard for years in a sport that I loved, had come through regional and national trials to achieve the dream of being selected to represent my country, only to be told by my college principal that my sport was not to be taken seriously. How I stopped myself from losing my temper I don't know. It was probably that I knew that this would completely ruin any chance that I might have of being given permission to go. Instead, I tried to explain to her how the game was developing into a serious competitive sport for females and what an honour it would be for the college to have an England international as one of its students. She did not appear to be convinced and dismissed me from her presence without a firm answer but with the promise that she would let me know her decision once she had consulted the college governors!

I left the house in a state of shock. I was really worried that I was going to be denied my big chance. I walked around in agonising limbo for several days until I happened to bump into the principal on the steps of the administration building. She beckoned me to approach her and introduced me with great enthusiasm to a man in a suit who was accompanying her. He turned out to be a football-mad college governor, who thought that it was fantastic that I had been selected to play for England and had been dying to meet me. I have always been a great believer in the saying 'it is better to be born lucky than rich'!

Needless to say I got my leave of absence and several weeks later I was on a train bound for London to meet up with the rest of the squad in preparation for the inaugural official England women's football international match.

three

On Tour With England

SCOTLAND, 18/11/1972: RAVENSCRAIG STADIUM, GREENOCK

Our very first England tour was a fantastic experience. We were to stay at Bisham Abbey National Sports Centre and play an exhibition match at the *Daily Express* Five-a-Side competition at Empire Pool, Wembley, prior to travelling to Scotland for the first ever official England international match. On the day of the *Daily Express* competition, which attracted top men's teams from the old First Division, the WFA had set-up a press photo-shoot at Wembley Stadium, where we would get the opportunity to train on the hallowed turf.

Unlike many of the girls, I had been to Wembley before as a spectator both at England women's hockey internationals and at the 1970 FA Cup final between Leeds United and Chelsea. I had never imagined then, however, that I would one day be welcomed into its inner sanctum. To change in the dressing rooms that had played host to so many legendary cup final teams and to take the famous walk up the tunnel and out on to the Wembley pitch was a dream come true for a football-mad eighteen-year-old. Representatives of the national press were there to take photographs and they were even invited into the changing rooms as the whole affair had created quite a lot of media interest.

It felt fantastic to be actually kicking the ball around on such a prestigious surface. I can remember looking outwards at the empty stands and trying to imagine what it would be like to play in the stadium when it was full of thousands of cheering people. The press were lined up at the side of the pitch, clamouring for photographs. They wanted some action shots and were suggesting various poses. Some of us were feeling rather self-conscious as we had been given very close-fitting shorts to wear, which were not the kind that we would normally play in. I am not sure who had provided these, or whether or not they were designed to have 'the Sepp Blatter effect'. Sepp Blatter is the current FIFA president who, in January 2004, was reported to have suggested that female players should wear skimpy kit, like women's beach volleyball teams, in order to make the game a more popular spectator sport! What I can point out, however, is that in the first official England team photograph, taken on the Wembley pitch that day, I have pulled my shirt right down over my shorts in an effort to cover the offending garment! Nonetheless, it was a wonderful and unforgettable experience and when we left the Wembley turf after a short training session, I stooped to pick some grass to keep for posterity.

That evening we rubbed shoulders with the rich and famous at the *Daily Express* Five-a-Side National Football Championship at the Empire Pool, Wembley. Or should I say rubbed knees? One of my friends in the team, Julia Brunton (née Manning) recalls literally brushing knees with George Best as she moved along the row to get to her reserved seat in the players' section. Later, as she was excitedly recounting this experience to her boyfriend, from a telephone booth in the foyer, she was interrupted by an urgent tapping on the glass. 'I looked up and found myself face to face with one of my all-time heroes,' she remembers. 'I quickly finished my conversation by saying: "I've got to go now. Geoff Hurst wants to use the phone!"'

We were able to mingle freely among all the players as we moved around the arena. Our dressing room was on the same corridor as those allocated to the men's teams. It was obviously a novelty for the men to have female players in their midst and it was easy to strike up a conversation. Celebrities that I chatted to and collected autographs from that evening included Mick Channon and Eric Martin, who were playing for Southampton; Colin Todd, John O'Hare, Alan Hinton and John McGovern (Derby County); Jon Sammels and Keith Weller (Leicester City); Mike Summerbee and Tony Book (Manchester City); Bruce Rioch (Aston Villa) and Dave Webb (Chelsea). They were all very supportive, curious to see us perform and interested to hear about our forthcoming international match.

The semi-finalists of the competition were West Ham, Ipswich, Derby County and Tottenham, with Ipswich and Tottenham contesting the final. Tottenham went on to lift the trophy. In the interval before the final, ten players from our squad played an exhibition match (England 'A' versus England 'B') in front of what was a very large audience. I was disappointed not to be selected for this game but this was compensated for by the fact that I was chosen by the WFA representatives to be interviewed for a television news programme, which was reporting on the event for one of the major channels. This was my first experience in front of a television camera. I was terrified but proud to be chosen and determined to perform well. Fortunately I was able to alert my family to what was happening. There were no video recorders in those days, so my father recorded my efforts by filming the television set with his cine camera!

The players who performed in the exhibition match were very nervous as they took centre stage, keen to impress and unsure of the reception that they might receive. The crowd did appear to be a bit sceptical at the outset (probably because most people at that time had yet to witness a women's football match) but the mood soon changed to surprised appreciation at the realisation that we could actually play a bit! The team put on a great display of skilful five-a-side football and came off at the end to generous applause from the audience and the receipt of genuine plaudits from the professionals. It was great publicity for the women's game in general and the new England team in particular.

Having spent that night (Wednesday 15 November) at Bisham Abbey National Sports Centre, we awoke on the Thursday morning to the prospect of a full day of training prior to departing on the Friday to travel to Scotland. Heading down for breakfast, we had the first real opportunity to take in our surroundings. Bisham Abbey is situated on the Thames, near Marlow in leafy Buckinghamshire. The main building, which we were staying in, is like an old stately home, all oak panelling and sweeping staircases. Outside, neatly manicured lawns lead right down to the river, where the well-heeled cruise past in their luxury boats. Equally well-kept, luxuriant grass football pitches have been blended into this landscape. I can remember being suitably impressed with the facilities!

After breakfast, we collected our boots and made our way out on to the field for our first proper training session. The squad was made up of schoolgirls, students, clerks, shorthand typists, machine operators, a clerical supervisor and a housewife. Our ages ranged from fifteen to twenty-eight and we had been drawn from all parts of the country. Eric Worthington, the lone man in the party, was charged with the task of moulding us into a team capable of taking on international opposition. He had one day to do it in!

Eric had fortunately had the chance to do some limited work with us at the trials weekend in Loughborough the previous September, and had wisely selected a squad with a strong nucleus of players from leading clubs and a blend of youth and experience. He had chosen a quartet of players (Sue Buckett, Lynda Hale, Pat Davies and Maggie Kirkland) from arguably the leading side in the country, Southampton Ladies. At that time they were the Manchester United of the women's game, having already won the Mitre Cup (the Women's FA Cup) for several years running and topped their league. A close-knit group, they were confident and professional in their approach. Sue Buckett, at twenty-eight years old, was their highly experienced goalkeeper. Eric chose her to be the backbone of the England team, a role she was to fulfil for many years. She was a supremely agile shot stopper, decisive on crosses and prepared to marshal her defence with calm authority. Lynda Hale was a flying right winger who could cross with precision, often on to the head of her teammate Pat Davies, who was a centre forward with a clinical finish. Maggie Kirkland (now Pearson) the final member of the Southampton quartet was, at fifteen, the youngest member of the England squad. She was already an accomplished overlapping full-back who was on the team sheet to start the Scotland game.

One of the other leading club sides of the time was Foden Ladies from Cheshire. They had played as an unofficial England team against the Scottish club champions (Westhorn United) in the international television final of Hughie Green's Butlin's Cup in 1970. Eric Worthington had included three Foden Ladies in his squad: Sheila Parker, Sylvia Gore and Jeannie Allott. Sheila Parker was a hard-tackling centre-back. Twenty-four years old and married with a young son, she was made the first ever captain of an official England women's team and kept us all in order! Her club-mate, Sylvia Gore, was the most experienced player in the England squad. At twenty-eight, she had four-teen years of football experience behind her and was a skilful inside forward. Between them, Sheila and Sylvia tried to mentor the third and youngest mem-ber of the Foden's team, sixteen-year-old schoolgirl Jeannie Allott. This was no easy task. Jeannie was a real live wire who, like me, found it hard to sit still. We were to become good friends and two of the jokers of the squad. Jeannie was a fantastic attacking midfielder who operated down the left-hand side of the pitch. She played with her long blonde hair loose and flowing and had, as a result, already commanded most of the press attention at the Wembley photo-shoot the previous day. This was to become a familiar pattern!

Another player that Eric had chosen to add to this talented bunch was Paddy McGroarty, who was my teammate at Thame. As I mentioned previously, she was a brilliant midfield player with attacking flair who combined excellent dribbling skills with a terrier-like tenacity. She was like George Best and Paul Gascgoine rolled into one! While Paddy had the attacking flair, no midfield would be complete without its defensive stopper. Janet Bagguley from Buxton was picked to fill this role. She was as hard as nails and a ferocious tackler.

With these nine players at the centre of his strategy, the manager spent the day on the training ground trying out possible permutations for the remaining places in the team, as well as familiarising us with the routines that he wanted to implement at attacking and defending set plays. We all worked extremely hard, desperate to impress in order to have the best chance of being selected to play in the match on the Saturday. After tea and a film analysis session, we spent the evening relaxing and packing our suitcases in readiness for an early start the next day.

We set off at 7.30 a.m. on Friday 17 November to head north, by coach, for our international game. I was thrilled to be going all the way to Scotland as I hadn't really travelled that much before. As one of the youngsters of the team (at eighteen) and still very green, I looked to older members of the squad for advice. Paddy McGroarty, our talented midfield general, was twenty-four and as a member of my club team Thame Ladies I looked up to her. She was a real character who was always game for a laugh. The press had got hold of the story that Paddy had once been a novice nun and she had agreed to pose for publicity photos dressed in a nun's habit. These were published in the *Sun* newspaper. Needless to say this didn't go down too well with those who were concerned about the image of the fledgling women's game. Anyway, Paddy was also very Scottish, although she apparently had some qualification (either place of birth or relative) that allowed her to play for England. So I trusted her judgement on all matters to do with travelling to her native land. As we approached the Scottish border, she came walking down the bus towards me with her passport in her hand and said to me, 'Wendy, get your passport out ready. We are coming to the border and you will need to show it or they won't let you in.' I immediately went into an absolute panic. I said that I didn't have my passport with me and I didn't realise that I had to bring it. The other girls sitting near me realised what was going on straight away and joined in on the joke. They all said, 'Haven't you brought it Wendy? You won't be allowed in to the country without it. You are going to have to get off the bus and go back.' I felt devastated – my dreams of playing for my country were about to be shattered because I had stupidly not realised and failed to pack my passport. The rotten lot kept it going for a good five minutes before they put me out of my misery.

When I had received my letter from the WFA secretary, Patricia Gregory, telling me the arrangements for the Scotland match, it had included strict instructions to bring a skirt as the hotel that we were booked into in Scotland (in Gourock, on the banks of the Clyde) didn't allow women to wear trousers! We were never sure whether this was actually true, or if the WFA officials had made it up to make sure that we looked smart! Anyway, this didn't go down too well with the players, most of whom, like me, were never out of trousers. I didn't even possess a dress or skirt and had to go out and buy one before I joined the tour.

Because of this rule my group of friends in the team and I spent most of the time in the hotel in someone's room, where we could relax in our shorts and play cards. Like the England men's team on tour, we found that we had quite a lot of time on our hands, so a group of us formed a card school to while away the hours. The group included sixteen-year-old Jeannie Allott, from Foden's, and seventeen-year-old Janet Bagguley, from Buxton. They were lively pair who, like me, were always looking for some fun. We only played for pennies though, it was all very harmless.

When it was time to board the coach to go to training or the game, we all dutifully marched through the hotel foyer in our skirts with our trousers packed into our bags. As soon as we got on to the coach, off came the skirts and

8th November 1972

Dear Wendy

    Since my earlier letter this week I have been in contact with the gentleman who is arranging the hotel booking for us and he informs me that he has been requested by the hotel in Scotland to make our party aware of one or two points. The first and most important is that dresses (or skirts) will be worn in the hotel by the female members of our party. This does not only refer to meal times. I realise that this will hit some of you quite hard in that you seem to have been born and bred in trousers! However, the hotel is large and caters for wedding receptions etc. and we do not want to upset anyone, least of all a bride. The other request is that you refrain from walking round the hotel in football kit. This is an unnecessary request as I am sure you would have the good manners not to walk into dinner in your muddy football gear.

    I now recall that I never mentioned money. You will not be expected to pay for anything except your personal bits and pieces which you might like to purchase i.e. the odd packet of crisps or bar of chocolate. You simply have to get yourself to Paddington Station on the 15th get some lunch somewhere and then get yourself home from wherever we drop you off. Unless you intend to drink yourself silly with Scottish whisky - and I can assure you we aren't paying for that - you just need to supply yourself with enough cash to keep your personal wishes going.

    Please bear the first paragraph of this letter in mind when packing for the five days. Let me know if you have any problems.

Yours sincerely,

Pat Gregory

P.S.   There will be a get-together with the Scots after the match. The game kicks-off at 2.15 p.m.

No trousers in the hotel! Strict instructions from the WFA for the Scotland match, November 1972.

a frantic change of clothes would take place as we were driving along. Goodness knows what any Scottish passers-by made of this. The same procedure would happen in reverse as we approached the hotel on the way back from the training ground. In all the rush, you were lucky not to end up wearing someone else's skirt when you got off the bus. If we were set up by the WFA management, then they certainly had a perverse sense of humour!

On the Saturday (18 November 1972) we travelled to Ravenscraig Stadium in Greenock to play the first official England women's international match. I still have the match programme, which is signed by all the players and the manager Eric Worthington. It was an auspicious occasion but I was feeling bitterly disappointed at not being selected for the starting eleven. I was to spend the match huddled up on the bench under a blanket, as the match was played out in icy conditions. To add insult to injury it began to snow heavily on us in the second half! Although it was not my day personally (my debut would come in the next international match in France the following April) the match was very close and exciting and, after being two goals to one down at half-time, I was delighted when our team just managed to clinch a three goals to two victory, with one goal from Pat Davies and two from Sylvia Gore. Sylvia had the distinction of scoring the very first goal for England, which has put her into the history books.

Programme for the first official women's international football match to be played in Great Britain, 18/11/72, signed by the England players and the England manager, Eric Worthington. England beat Scotland 3-2.

SCOTLAND

Colours: Navy/White, White Pants, Red Stockings

HOUGHTON

HUNTER   HUNTER

KIDD   MOUNT   WALKER

REILLY   NEILLIS   ANDERSON   McAULAY   CARR
(Capt.)

Substitutes: Creamer, Davenport, Cooper, McLaren, Morrison

I would like to extend a warm welcome to our English guests this afternoon and hope that their visit to Scotland may be an enjoyable one.

This being the first ever International between the two countries, I hope we shall have a good sporting game and be able to make this event an annual affair.

R. STEWART, Scotland Team Manager.

SCOTTISH TEAM

Scotland are captained today by Inside Left MARGARET McAULAY (21), of Westthorn Utd. of Hamilton. Brilliant midfield player, but prefers to bang in the goals.

JANIE HOUGHTON (17), of Cambuslang Hooverettes, is our goalkeeper and though rather short in stature for a keeper, is very agile and quick.

JEAN HUNTER (17), part of the midfield trio of the successful Lees Ladies. Strong tackler and very able to take on a player or two by herself.

JUNE HUNTER (19) is a very versatile player and can turn out in almost any position. Plays for Motherwell A.E.I. and is today at Left Back.

LINDA KIDD (21), also of Lees Ladies. Linda comes from Kilmarnock. Good distributor of the ball and helps start many a dangerous attack.

MARIAN MOUNT (18), Centre Half, plays for Westthorn Utd. Marion hails from Greenock so should be quite confident playing in front of her home crowd.

SANDRA WALKER (22), of Lees Ladies, is married and has two young children. Sandra has it all, brilliant ball control, strong tackler, good header and the stylish arrogance of a Jim Baxter.

ROSE REILLY (17), perhaps the best-known of the Scots girls. Joint top goal-scorer with the speed necessary in a winger and a terrific shot. Began her playing career when only 7 years old for her local team Stewarton Thistle (now Lees Ladies). Has since joined Westthorn Utd.

EDNA NEILLIS (18). Brilliant ball-control and fantastic finish. Likened by many to "Jinky" Johnstone of Celtic, which doesn't please Edna as she's a Rangers fanatic. A real character, joint top goal-scorer, plays for Westthorn Utd., easily distinguished by her red hair.

MARY ANDERSON (18) also plays Centre Forward for her club, Westthorn Utd. Brilliant opportunist in front of goal.

MARY CARR (20) plays on the left wing for her club, Motherwell A.E.I., and lives in Hamilton.

LIZ CREAMER (19), substitute goalkeeper, plays for Dundee Strikers.

MARY DAVENPORT (20), stocky defender who gives full ninety minutes. Plays for Westthorn Utd. and lives in Dunfermline.

LINDA COOPER (16) is the youngest member of the team. Turns out at Centre Forward for her club, Dundee Strikers.

DIANE McLAREN (17), also of Dundee Strikers, packs a strong shot and doesn't waste many chances.

IRENE MORRISON (24), strong defender, usually plays Centre Half for her club, Motherwell A.E.I. Lets opponents know they've been in a game.

ROBERT STEWART, Scottish Manager and former professional footballer with Kilmarnock and St. Mirren.

Scotland team for the first international women's football match, England v. Scotland, 18/11/72.

ENGLAND

Colours: White, Navy Shorts, White Stockings

BUCKETT

KIRKLAND   GRAHAM

BAGGULEY   PARKER   M'GROARTY
(Capt.)

HALE   GORE   DAVIES   ALLOTT   WILSON

Substitutes: Owen, Manning, Foreman, Whyatt

Even before the formation of the Women's Football Association in 1969 the aim of the organisers was to promote women's football at International level. We now see the realisation of this aim with today's game. The England squad were selected from regional competitions and final trials, and at a training weekend the present squad were selected.   ERIC WORTHINGTON, England Manager.

ENGLISH TEAM

SHEILA PARKER (24), Centre Half and Captain from Fodens L.F.C. Housewife with young son.

JEANNIE ALLOTT (16). This blond striker also stars with Fodens and is a brilliant opportunist.

JANET BAGGULEY (17). From Buxton and plays for Macclesfield L.F.C.

SUE BUCKETT (28). Southampton keeper for five years. Toured America two years ago. One of the most experienced keepers in the game in England.

PAT (Thunder) DAVIES (17). Also from the crack Southampton team and earned her nickname for her shooting power.

EILEEN FOREMAN (18). A prolific goal scorer from Warminster in the West Country.

SYLVIA GORE (28). The most experienced player in the side, with 14 years of football behind her; a crafty inside forward from Fodens L.F.C.

SANDRA GRAHAM (28). A hard-tackling left back who lives and plays in Blackpool.

LYNDA HALE (18). Also with Southampton L.F.C., a strong and determined Outside Right.

MORAG KIRKLAND (15), youngest of the side and the fourth member from Southampton L.F.C.

JULIA MANNING (21), lives and plays in Lowestoft. Also plays representative Hockey.

PADDY M'GROARTY (25). Cousin of Pat Crerand, English born, but lived for many years in Scotland. Reckoned to be the George Best of Ladies' Football.

WENDY OWEN (18). "The Joker" in the pack, but takes her football seriously, presently a student.

SUSAN WHYATT (16), from Macclesfield and is reserve keeper.

JEAN WILSON (23), from Manchester Corinthians, and a bank clerk.

ERIC WORTHINGTON, Manager. F.A. coach, Senior Lecturer at Loughborough College. Is former professional player and is responsible for team selection.

Referee: Mr. J .CLELLAND (Glasgow)

Linesmen: Mr. D. MUNRO, Mr. J. GIBB (both East Kilbride)

In attendance: The Renfrewshire & Bute Police Pipe Band

England team for the first international women's football match, England v. Scotland, 18/11/72.

FRANCE, 22/4/1973: BRION STADIUM, BRION, NEAR CHATEAUROUX

The moment that I had been dreaming of for years, walking on to the pitch to play for England, came in April 1973 against France. By then Eric Worthington, who was only to manage the England team for the first international, had been lured to Australia as director of coaching.

John Adams, the FA northern regional coach, took control of the squad on a temporary basis until a more permanent replacement could be found. His approach to fitness training was novel. Arriving fit to play was each individual's responsibility, as we usually only came together just before a match. Prior to the France game, I received a letter from the WFA informing me that the manager had decided that he would institute a regime whereby at the very first training session on our meeting as a squad for a match, the players would have to do a set number of repetitions of shuttle runs. Anyone who couldn't complete them would not be selected in the starting eleven. This did give you a great incentive to train before the trip. I can remember being out pounding the streets at night and practising by myself on a makeshift shuttle circuit to build up my repetitions!

My first England game, against France (away), 22/4/73.

The team gathered at Lea Green National Sports Centre in Derbyshire for a day's training in England before leaving for France. As soon as we had unpacked and settled in we were taken out on to the training ground for the fitness test. In my memory most players managed to complete it but there were a few players who disappeared to throw up in the hedge afterwards!

Our preparations on home soil complete, we travelled to Brion, near Chateauroux, where we found that we were to be accommodated in a girls' boarding school. We slept in dormitories that were off a corridor with only a curtain to pull across. Two rows of beds faced each other down each of the side walls of the room. Even the WFA officials had to sleep together in a dorm. They were not impressed with the accommodation!

After the disappointment of being on the substitutes' bench for the Scotland match, I was overjoyed to be picked in the starting eleven against France. Julia Manning, who had kept me company on that occasion, was also to get her first start. John Adams was giving me the chance to demonstrate my capabilities when he picked me in the centre of the defence to play alongside the captain, Sheila Parker. I was really nervous in the dressing room before the game. The situation was not aided by the fact that the toilet facilities at the Stadium de Brion were typically French: a hole in the ground with footplates on either side!

The first time that you line up to sing the National Anthem before playing for your country is a bit special and it certainly brought a tear to my eye. Looking around at the crowd of 3,000 spectators, which was good attendance for a women's international, did little to calm the butterflies in my stomach. Once the game kicked off my nerves began to disappear, however, and I was just keen to put in a good performance to consolidate my place in the team. In the end we ran out comfortable winners, putting three goals past the French. Eileen Foreman came off the subs bench to score one of them in what was her debut game and Pat Davies got the other two. Perhaps more importantly from my perspective, we kept a clean sheet at our end. I must have made a reasonably good impression on my debut because from that France game onwards I became first choice centre-back alongside Sheila Parker. We complimented each other well. My main strength was my heading ability, so I dealt with most of the threats in the air, while Sheila's tenacious tackling stopped anyone trying to break through on the ground.

After the France match we were treated to a five-course official banquet that contributed to our culinary education. We were completely fazed by the French way of serving a meal, however. When they brought around the plates with the meat on, as a separate course, we were all sitting waiting for the potatoes and vegetables to arrive. When we got back to our dorm, one of our number was very ill (a combination of rich French food and a little too much red wine). The only receptacle that we could find for her to be sick into was one of the fire buckets that were hanging on the wall at the entrance to the dorm. To compound our problem, for some reason, best known to the French, these had rounded bottoms and if placed on the ground would roll from side to side like a 'weeble'. This was not too handy under the circumstances and I remember performing the extremely delicate manoeuvre of holding on to my colleague with one hand and the bucket with the other. Not an easy feat when you have had a few glasses of wine yourself!

Generally we enjoyed a lot more freedom to celebrate after matches than I believe is the case with the current England team on tour. We were on a strict curfew on the night before a game, which we respected as we were serious about our football and proud to be representing our country. There was always some sort of do afterwards, however, which was usually attended by both players and officials. On these occasions, as long as we didn't go overboard, we could let our hair down.

I remember one particular post-match event that was held in a large room with a stage. Being a bit of a performer (I get it from my father who is a talented Welsh tenor) I got up on the stage and sang a song. I can't remember what, probably an Elvis number. I gave it the full hit and ended the performance by diving off the stage full length into the outstretched arms of the team, who had formed two parallel lines and joined their arms across as a landing net. Nowadays that would be a recognised activity on one of those expensive team-building weekends!

SCOTLAND, 23/6/1973: NUNEATON BOROUGH FC

John Adams was sadly only in charge of the England team for two matches (the 3-0 away win over France in April 1973 and the 8-0 home win over Scotland in June of that year). He was a superb coach, with a wry sense of humour. As Sue Lopez mentioned in her book *Women on the Ball* (1997), he did tell me to remember that I couldn't play football and to concentrate on what I was good at: stopping the opposition from playing!

He was a great psychologist in the days before the importance of this aspect was widely recognised within football circles as being important for optimum performance. His ideas in this area were, I believe, instrumental in our total annihilation of the Scots in his second and final game in charge. What he managed to do before the game was to totally convince us that we were going to be so superior that we couldn't fail. He used a very interesting method to achieve this. On the coach on the way to the game, he brought around a crate of a new energy drink. This was before the days when these became widely available and routinely drunk by sportspeople as a nutritional aid. In fact, none of us had ever heard of this idea before. He convinced us that by drinking this concoction we

THE WOMEN'S
FOOTBALL ASSOCIATION

presents

ENGLAND

v.

SCOTLAND

on

Saturday 23rd June 1973

at

Nuneaton Borough F.C.

Nuneaton

Kick-off 3 p.m.

PROGRAMME 5p.

The first England home match, 23/6/73. We beat Scotland 8-0!

were going to have so much more energy than the Scots that we would be able to run them into the ground. This is exactly what happened and we went on to put eight goals past the them with no reply. I can remember feeling so full of running right until the final whistle, which just goes to show the power of mind over matter (or was it in reality all those shuttle runs?). I don't think that we had ever won an international by such a wide margin before, or ever repeated the feat again during the period that I was playing for the team.

That Scotland game was also notable because it was the first England women's international match to be played on home soil. The manager used it as an opportunity to try out some new young players. One of these was Pat Firth (from Fleece Fillies and later Foden's) who made her debut as a striker only a short while after her sixteenth birthday. She won't forget that day because she scored a hat-trick! The other goal-scorers were Pat Davies (2), Paddy McGroarty (2) and Eileen Foreman (1). Pat Firth, along with Pat Davies, was to become one of our most prolific strikers over the next few years.

Another debutant in the Scotland game was seventeen-year-old schoolgirl Maggie Miks from Coventry Bantams, who came in as right-back. She and I were to become firm friends over the next few years. We now had two Maggie's playing in defence, as Maggie Pearson, née Kirkland, who had been in the side from the very beginning, played at left-back. They were both hard-tackling, overlapping full-backs of the highest quality and, together with myself and Sheila Parker, formed a formidable back four that was well supported and bossed by our goalkeeper Sue Buckett. She kept us all in order in a calm and

ENGLAND v. SCOTLAND

A very warm welcome to you all today on the occasion of England's first "home" International. This afternoon's game is, in fact, England's third International and its second against Scotland.

The first official International played in Great Britain was held on November 18th, 1972, at Greenock between Scotland and England. The weather was bitter, the pitch icy, and half of the match was played in a snowstorm.

At half-time Scotland were winning by two goals to one, but two second-half goals enabled England to win the match by three goals to two.

At Easter this year England played France at Brion, near Châteauroux, in France, and in front of 3,000 French spectators beat the home side by three goals to nil.

The England Squad named on the opposite page was selected after a series of trials which were based on an Inter-League representative team competition for the Lillywhites Trophies. Each of the W.F.A.'s registered leagues was invited to enter a representative team and nineteen took up the challenge. By splitting the leagues into Northern and Southern groups and devoting a whole day to finding the top league in each area we gave the England manager the opportunity of seeing about 300 of the best players in this country. On 3rd June the title of the top English Inter-League team was won by the Home Counties League who beat the Heart of England League 5-0 at Evesham, Worcestershire.

From the 300 girls, 15 were selected to play the existing England Squad at a Final Trial held in Nottingham and from that afternoon the new Squad of 17 was chosen.

Scotland, in comparison, have a mere handful of clubs from which to choose their International players and it is a tribute to the skill and tenacity of the Scots that they are able to give the English clubs and International Side such hard-fought games.

The manager of the England Squad at the time of its inauguration was Eric Worthington and he was with us for only the first International match, against Scotland. At the beginning of this year he was appointed to take overall charge of soccer coaching in Australia. In recognition of his short time with us Eric has presented the W.F.A. with the handsome trophy which is to be won for the first time today and which will be the prize each time our two countries meet in the future.

Thank you for your support and good luck to both teams.

Excerpt from the match programme.

ENGLAND SQUAD	SCOTLAND SQUAD
Colours: White shirts Blue shorts White socks	Colours: Navy & White shirts White shorts Red socks
JEANNIE ALLOTT Foden.	**GERRY CHALMERS** Lees Ladies.
JANET BAGGULEY Macclesfield.	**SUSAN FERRIES** Lees Ladies.
SUSAN BUCKETT Southampton.	**LINDA KIDD** Lees Ladies.
PAT DAVIES Southampton.	**ROSE REILLY** Westthorn Utd.
PAT FIRTH Fleece Fillies.	**EDNA NEILLIS** Westthorn Utd.
EILEEN FOREMAN Warminster.	**MARY ANDERSON** Westthorn Utd.
SYLVIA GORE Foden.	**MARGARET McAULAY** Westthorn Utd.
LYNDA HALE Southampton.	**LIZ CREAMER** Dundee Strikers.
MORAG KIRKLAND Southampton.	**JUNE HUNTER** Motherwell A.E.I.
SUSAN LOPEZ Southampton.	**MARY CARR** Motherwell A.E.I.
JULIA MANNING Lowestoft.	**SHEILA BEGBIE** Edinburgh Dynamo.
MARGARET McGROARTY Thame.	**MARGARET WILSON** Edinburgh Dynamo.
MARGARET MIKS Coventry Bantams.	**ANN MORRISON** Aberdeen Prima Donnas.
WENDY OWEN Thame.	**MARLYN GAVIN** Fife Dynamites.
SHEILA PARKER Foden.	
LESLEY STIRLING Preston North End.	
SUSAN WHYATT Macclesfield.	
Manager: JOHN ADAMS.	

Team line-ups for England v. Scotland at Nuneaton, 23/6/73.

authoritative manner while making fantastic agile saves to stop anyone that did manage to get through.

Our record as a defensive unit speaks for itself. In the seven internationals that we played in together (from June 1973 to April 1975) we only conceded two goals. We were aided, of course, by all the talented players that we had in front of us, who kept the ball away from us and were consistent in scoring at the other end!

After the Scotland match we had to say goodbye to John Adams, who had been our second manager in the space of a year. His record of two wins in two matches, with eleven goals for and none against would be a hard act to follow.

Our new manager was Tommy Tranter. Tommy was manager of Slough Town, a team that played in the Isthmian League. He was also a lecturer in physical education at Borough Road College, which was one of the top PE colleges at that time. An excellent coach, Tommy enabled us to continue our winning streak. His period of stewardship began with a run of three home wins against Northern Ireland, the Netherlands and Wales.

The Northern Ireland game, which we won 5–1 at Bath City on 7 September 1973 was notable for being the first international women's match to be played under floodlights. It also saw the England debut of Sue Lopez from Southampton, who was a brilliant attacking midfielder and another member of the Southampton Ladies team. She was destined to achieve great honours for her work in women's football, which I will speak more about later in the book.

Our 1-0 victory against the Netherlands was achieved at Elm Park (then home of Reading FC) on 9 November 1973. This was an even more historic occasion in that it was the first ever official women's international match to be played on a professional League ground, since the lifting of the 1921 FA ban. This caused quite a stir in the press and photographers and reporters came to take photographs of us training at Bisham Abbey on the day of the game.

THE NETHERLANDS, 31/5/1974: STADSPARK STADIUM, GRONINGEN

Our first away tour under Tommy Tranter's management was to be the return fixture against the Netherlands at Groningen in Holland. This time we beat them by the even wider margin of three goals to nil.

After the match we were given some free time in Amsterdam 'to go shopping'. For me and my friends this seemed like an opportunity not to be missed, so we duly set off to seek some entertainment. Where else would a group of young people let loose in Amsterdam head for but the famous red-light district? We didn't have a clue how to get there, so we decided to hop on a tram and ask directions as we went. The trouble was that none of us spoke any Dutch or even knew the name of the area that we were headed for. This didn't turn out to be a problem however; we just approached passers-by and said, 'Sex Street?' and Eureka! People's faces broke into a smile and we were guided all the way there. That's Amsterdam for you.

WOMEN'S FOOTBALL ASSOCIATION

ENGLAND

v.

THE NETHERLANDS

FRIDAY, 9th NOVEMBER, 1973

KICK-OFF 7.30 p.m.

READING FOOTBALL CLUB

ELM PARK, NORFOLK ROAD, READING

OFFICIAL PROGRAMME 5p

First England match to be played on a professional ground, 9/11/73. England beat the Netherlands 1-0.

We walked around the red-light district with our mouths wide open. We couldn't believe how upfront and non-seedy it was. It was like a tourist area, pleasant and relaxed with a canal running through and boats meandering past. Bars and eating places stood shoulder to shoulder with the main business of the district. Women were openly plying their trade, either displaying themselves in shop windows or standing outside in what appeared to be their allotted positions. We sat for a while in a bar opposite a house of ill repute and took bets on how long it would be from the time that a man walked into the building, having made some sort of transaction, until the time that he re-emerged. The record was about one-and-a-half minutes!

We had a great time, which was all very educational, and were back at our hotel at the specified time with no-one any the wiser as to how we had spent our afternoon off.

FRANCE, 7/11/1974: WIMBLEDON FC, PLOUGH LANE

For our next game, which was a 2-0 home win against France, several players appeared in the match programme for the first time. These included Sandra Choat, a talented forward from QPR; Liz Deighan (Fodens), an excellent attacking midfielder; Carol Thomas (née McCune) from Hull Brewery, who came on as a substitute to make her debut at right-back. Liz and Carol were both to go on to make their mark on the women's game.

After a few games as a substitute, Carol soon made the right-back position her own and was to go on to have a long and distinguished England career. Her name can be found in the *Guinness Book of Records* as the first woman to be capped fifty times for England at football. Carol also went on to become England's second captain (taking over from Sheila Parker at the Pony Home International Championships in 1976) and was to lead the side forty-nine times in a fantastic fifty-six-cap career.

Liz Deighan was also to enjoy a distinguished playing career. Like Carol, she was a member of the England team that finished runners-up in the 1984 European Championship. After retiring as a player Liz went into coaching and in 1987 became coach to the first England Under-21 team, which was in existence for four years between 1987 and 1992.

SWITZERLAND, 19/4/1975: BASLE

Our next away trip with England was to Basle in Switzerland, in April 1975. The Swiss game was played in front of a sizeable crowd at a magnificent stadium. We won 3-1 to bring our match statistics to nine consecutive victories. It was Carole Thomas's first away trip with England and, in common with many of the England players when they first travelled away with the team, her first trip abroad. She remembers being impressed by the posh hotel that we stayed in near the centre of the town, where all of our rooms had balconies. Since the dormitory experience on our first trip to France, the accommodation that we had enjoyed on our overseas visits had been very good. My most enduring memory of that trip, however, is how expensive it was to buy anything over there. A group of us visited a bar in the evening after the game and could only afford to buy one beer at a time, which five of us shared by sipping slowly through straws!

SWEDEN, 15/6/1975: ULLEVI STADIUM, GOTHENBURG

In June 1975 we travelled to Sweden for the first ever match between our two countries. Making her debut for England in that game was Elaine Badrock (or Baddie, as she was always called) who played her club football for Prestatyn in North Wales. Baddie was a tall, powerful centre forward who was to form an effective strike partnership with Pat Firth and go on to play fourteen times for her country. She also became my good friend and room-mate for the rest of my time in the England team.

Baddie was going to have to wait a while to get on the scoresheet for England, however, as Sweden ended our unbeaten run of nine successive victories over two-and-a-half years by beating us 2-0 in the fantastic Ullevi Stadium in Gothenburg. They had a team of players who were fitter and more athletic-looking, as well as more skilful than us. I can remember being really impressed, not just by the stadium (we often got to play in much bigger and better arenas on our travels in Europe than we ever did at home) but by the superior physiques of the Swedish forwards that I was unable to catch! Just to rub it in,

First England defeat: Sweden 2 England 0 (away), 15/6/75.

Program

Landskamp i fotboll damer
Sverige — England

ULLEVI
Söndagen den 15 juni 1975
kl. 18.00

they came over to England barely three months later, to beat us again by a margin of three goals to one.

This was our wake-up call. We had found a country that was more professional in its approach to the women's game than we were. Over the next twenty-five years, Scandinavian teams like Norway and Sweden, where women's football became fully integrated into the National Football Association in the 1970s, would go on to produce sides capable of challenging for honours at the highest level, while England would, in relative terms, be left behind.

PONY HOME INTERNATIONAL CHAMPIONSHIP, 22-23/5/1976

The disappointment at losing our unbeaten record was partly compensated for by our performances in the first Home International Championships in May 1976, the Pony Cup. This was a three-nation affair involving Wales, Scotland and England. For some reason Northern Ireland did not take part. The tournament, sponsored by Showerings, who produced Babycham and Pony wines, was to be played over a three-day period, during which we would meet Wales on 22 May at Bedford Town FC and Scotland at Enfield the following day. These venues were both the homes of semi-professional clubs.

We had a new captain for the tournament in the shape of Carol Thomas (née McCune) as Sheila Parker had not been named in the squad this time. Sheila went out of the picture for a while at this point. She had been one of the older members of the original England team who, like Paddy McGroarty and Sylvia Gore, were women for whom the England set-up came along rather late in their footballing careers. They were all great players who made a fantastic contribution to that first England team before giving way to the up-and-coming youngsters. Sheila did return to the team, however, at the age of thirty, just after I had retired. She scored the only goal in a fantastic 1-0 win against Italy at Wimbledon FC on 15 November 1977 and played on until 1980.

It was going to be strange for me not to be playing with Sheila. Our partnership at the centre of the defence had endured for ten successive internationals, since I had made my debut in France. During that time the team had only conceded seven goals. My new partner Linda Coffin was an excellent replacement, however, who was yet another player from the crack Southampton team. We were soon to develop an understanding and got on well together both on and off the field.

Another new name on the team sheet for the Home Internationals (and yet another player from Southampton Ladies) was nineteen-year-old Pat Chapman. She was a fantastic left winger who was a great crosser of the ball. She was to go on to make a big impression in the England team.

Because the Pony Home International Championship was the first tournament that an England women's team had participated in, quite a big fuss was

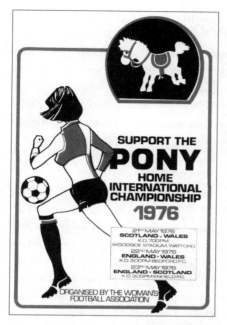

22nd MAY, 1976, BEDFORD TOWN F.C., BEDFORD	
ENGLAND	**WALES**
Colours: White Shirts / Blue Shorts	Colours: Red Shirts / White Shorts

ENGLAND		WALES
SUE BUCKETT	1	DIANNE TOTTY
CAROL McCUNE	2	GILLIAN MASKELL
MORAG KIRKLAND	3	KAREN WELLS
ALISON LEATHERBARROW	4	ANN JENKINS
WENDY OWEN	5	JAYNE ANGOVE
LINDA COFFIN	6	DEBBIE PEARSON
LORAINE DOBB	7	JULIE YALE
RAYNER HADDEN	8	LINDA JAMES
ELAINE BADROCK	9	SHELLEY WALTERS
PAT FIRTH	10	GLORIA O'CONNELL
PAT CHAPMAN	11	MAI GRIFFITH
KATHY HAMSTEAD	12	GILLIAN ROWLANDS
DEBBIE SMITH	13	
ANGELA POPPY	14	LESLEY JUDD
AUDREY RIGBY	15	SALLY MANLEY
	16	JUNE HOULDEY

REFEREE:
JOHN HUNTING

LINESMEN:
Red Flag: D. S. BONE
Yellow Flag: B. BELLAMY

MATCH BALL KINDLY DONATED BY MITRE SPORTS

Above left: First tournament match for an England team: England v. Wales, Pony Home International Championship, Bedford Town FC, 22/5/76. England won 4-0.

Above right: The teams for the first Home International match between England and Wales.

made of us. The sponsor had funded some smart white tracksuit tops that were emblazoned with its motif and had 'England' written large, right across the back. I can remember feeling very proud as we posed for publicity photographs wearing them. This was the first and only bit of kit that we were allowed to keep after an England game (apart from football boots, which were given to us by Mitre Sports for the very first England game) and I think that I wore it for weeks afterwards! On its very limited budget, the WFA couldn't normally afford to let us keep our kit, which they often had to beg, steal or borrow and return after a game. There was no help with kit from the FA, through the sponsors of the men's international team kit, like there is today.

When all the posing and preparations were over, we performed really well in both of our championship matches, beating Wales 4-0 and Scotland 5-1 to lift the trophy. The fact that England had gone on to win the first Home International Championship brought the team to the attention of the press and reports appeared in several papers the following day. Although the tournament wasn't apparently newsworthy enough to attract television coverage, my father did capture some of the action on cine film! This is a valuable record from an era where very little, if any, footage exists.

MEET THE TEAMS - ENGLAND

Name	Age	Club	Occupation
Sue Buckett	(31)	Southampton	*Clerical Supervisor*
Carol McCune	(20)	Hull	*Office Clerk*
Morag Kirkland	(18)	Southampton	*Student*
Alison Leatherbarrow	(20)	Prestatyn	*Sales Assistant*
Wendy Owen	(22)	Dartford College	*P.E. Teacher*
Linda Coffin	(20)	Southampton	*Section Manager*
Loraine Dobb	(16)	Rangers—Nottingham	*Schoolgirl*
Rayner Hadden	(21)	Droitwich St. Andrews	*Filament Producer*
Elaine Badrock	(20)	Prestatyn	*Packer*
Pat Firth	(18)	Doncaster Belles	*Production Worker*
Pat Chapman	(19)	Southampton	*Stock Controller*
Kathy Hamstead	(17)	Kilnhurst	*Student*
Debbie Smith	(15)	Preston North End	*Schoolgirl*
Angela Poppy	(22)	Lowestoft	*Cost Clerk*
Audrey Rigby	(18)	Rangers—Nottingham	*Clerk*

Manager: TOMMY TRANTER

In 1972 the very first England Squad of girls was selected, following a series of league, regional and national trials. The trials were specifically designed to give every girl who played football and was eligible, the opportunity of playing for England.

Each year, similar trials have been held, and it has been noticeable how many girls who, having failed to be selected, have worked at their game to improve their skills, and have come back one or two years later to be included in the squad. This annual search for fresh players makes sure that England always has, barring injuries, the best team available. In their 12 internationals to date, they are undefeated against teams from the British Isles, and have only suffered two defeats in Europe, both at the hands of Sweden.

PREVIOUS INTERNATIONAL RESULTS

Scotland	2	England	3	Holland	0	England	3
France	0	England	3	England	2	France	0
England	8	Scotland	0	Switzerland	1	England	3
England	5	N. Ireland	1	Sweden	2	England	0
England	1	Holland	0	England	1	Sweden	3
England	5	Wales	0	England	2	Holland	1

England team information from the Home International between England and Wales.

ITALY, 2 & 5/6/76: ROME AND CESENA

One month later, in June 1976, we went on what to us was a fabulous tour. We were off to Italy for a whole week, where we would play the Italian women's international team twice, firstly at the Olympic Stadium in Rome and later further south in Cesena, near Rimini.

I had managed to persuade the school that I was teaching at to give me leave of absence to play, but I know that some of the other players had to either take a week's holiday or unpaid leave from work to be able to go. There was no daily allowance for England players to compensate for lost wages like there is today. The WFA just couldn't afford it. Nevertheless, I am sure that at the time everyone thought that it was worth it for such a wonderful opportunity to enjoy a week away with the England squad on an all-expenses-paid trip.

We were really excited, as we were staying in the Olympic Village for the Rome game. This had been built to house the athletes for the 1960 Olympic Games. The village was beginning to look a bit on the shabby side but it had a wonderful outdoor pool and the weather was glorious. To be able to dive into the pool after a really hot training session was so refreshing.

The experience of playing in the Olympic Stadium in Rome was awesome. Women's football in Italy was far more advanced than in England. There was a semi-professional national league and the game was in general taken far more seriously and attracted a much wider audience. We had never before played in such a large and prestigious stadium and the nerves were visibly jangling in the dressing room. We had trained well the previous day and our manager did his best to calm us with his final team talk. Nothing, however, could have prepared us for our entry into the arena. Access to the pitch at the Olympic Stadium was via a steep set of stairs which suddenly brought us up and out into the centre of the arena. As we emerged into the open, we were met by the sound of nearly 10,000 people cheering and shouting for Italia. It was fantastic but also very intimidating. A large proportion of the crowd at one end were soldiers in uniform and there was a moat all around the pitch separating us from the chanting crowd. Having visited the Coliseum the previous day, the parallels between us and the early Christians did briefly cross my mind. The official attendance was apparently around 10,000 but to me it seemed more like 40,000. In England, women's international matches attracted a crowd of no more than 1,000-2,000 at that time. As we ran on to the pitch to start our warm-up, my heart was in my mouth. Given the circumstances, miles away from home, playing a far more experienced and professional side, in front of a hostile crowd, we acquitted ourselves very well.

After the nerves had settled we began to play good football, but were unable to break through against a very physical side. We eventually went down two goals to nil but it had been a brilliant experience. The Italian women defended just like their male counterparts and our centre forward Elaine Badrock (Baddie) had the bruises the next day to prove it. She was black and blue all down her spine and the backs of her legs. I had never seen anything like it before. Quite a few of our team had taken some knocks and our physio had her work cut out to get everyone fit for the hard battle that we knew we would face in Cesena, later in the week.

Before we left Rome for Cesena, our hosts had arranged for our team to have an audience with the Pope, at the Vatican. Looking back this was obviously a very special honour, but at the time I can remember being hugely disappointed. Again, being young and fairly naïve, I was under the misapprehension that an audience with the Pope meant a small private meeting, just us and him. Instead we had to sit for hours on a hard bench with hundreds of other people, while the Pope greeted a whole variety of groups from all over the world in their own language. The only part of the proceedings that we could understand was when he finally said, 'and welcome to the England women's football team' and that was it, our audience was over!

We were pleased to be moving on from Rome. The accommodation in the Olympic Village had been rather Spartan and the food not to our liking. Being typically English, we were very unadventurous when came to sampling the Italian cuisine and had eaten very little. On arrival in Cesena, we were delighted to find that we had been booked into a lovely hotel with en-suite facilities. The real treat, however, was the evening meal. Our hosts had decided to prepare an English meal of chicken and chips for us. They couldn't have made a better choice. Sixteen starving female footballers tucked in with real relish and they had to keep the chips flowing!

Our second match against the Italians proved to be a much closer affair. We had learnt lessons from the Rome game and managed to match our opponents, holding them to one goal each until the closing stages. Baddie had recovered sufficiently from her bruising encounter in Rome to score our only goal. In the last ten minutes, however, the Italians' superior strength and fitness allowed them to go on and score the decisive winner. Losing 2-1 away from home was no disgrace but it was very significant in that we had found another European side capable of beating us.

FRANCE, 26/2/77: PARIS

My last match for England (although I was unaware that this was to be the case at the time) was against France, in Paris, in February 1977. The previous October we had beaten Wales away at Ebbw Vale. I had high hopes for the trip as I thought that we would have an opportunity to go sightseeing in the city. Unfortunately this did not come to fruition. The tour was a short weekend affair where all we got to see was the airport, hotel, training ground and the stadium. My parents and sister decided to come over for the game and they got to see the sights that I didn't. The game, a goal-less draw, was also a bit of a damp squib and a rather disappointing end to what, for me, had been a fabulous England career.

Unfortunately I had to retire prematurely from playing for England due to injury. I was dropped from the squad for the first time following the game in Paris, but I was only twenty-three and should have had plenty of time to fight my way back in. I had been plagued by neck problems for several years but by now my condition was pretty bad. I suffered from chronic pain after club matches and had migraines that lasted the whole week until the next one. My everyday life was becoming severely affected. I couldn't sit comfortably in a chair and couldn't turn my head to speak to people next to me.

I am sure that my problems stemmed from too much heading of the ball in a match. My strength in the air was one of my main assets and the symptoms that I was experiencing were fairly typical for an old-fashioned centre half. I paid to see an osteopath and the WFA arranged for me to see an orthopaedic specialist at Charing Cross Hospital. Nothing seemed to help however, and I knew that my England days were over.

Although I retired from international football in 1977, I did manage to carry on playing club football for a few more years with Maidstone Ladies in the Kent League. I tried to play as a sweeper, dropping deep and leaving other people to head the ball. This wasn't terribly successful, however, and although I had a lot of fun with a great bunch of girls, I would have to say that as a player I was a shadow of my former self.

At Maidstone, however, I was fortunate to have the opportunity to play alongside a very young Debbie Bampton, who was just breaking into the England side (she gained her first cap against the Republic of Ireland in 1978). She was a hugely talented midfield player who went on to play for England for many years. Debbie became a great England captain, leading the team in the 1995 World Cup in Sweden, where we reached the quarter-finals: England's greatest achievement in this competition to date.

Looking back on my international career, I count myself lucky that I played football for England in what I believe to have been a golden age for the team; when we had some great players and were one of the top sides in Europe. This was before other nations caught us up by fully supporting the sport at a far earlier stage in its development in their country than we did in ours.

I had the privilege of being in at the very start of the England set-up and played under three excellent managers during a five-year period between November 1972 and February 1977. Apart from the two Home International Championship matches, all our games were friendlies. The first official European Championship did not take place until 1984 and the first World Cup until 1991. In the eighteen matches that I had been involved in, however, sixteen as a first-choice player and two as a sub, we had won thirteen, drawn one and lost four. We played matches against eight different countries and only lost to two, Italy and Sweden.

This was a very special period in my life, during which I learnt a lot more about 'the beautiful game', met some wonderful people, travelled to places I had previously only dreamt about and generally had a thoroughly great time. All of this was made possible by the work of some very dedicated people, including England managers Eric Worthington, John Adams and Tommy Tranter; physiotherapist Jane Talbot; team doctor Ernie Taylor; press officer Roger Ebben and a group of WFA officials who worked tirelessly in a completely voluntary capacity to organise the women's game. I don't think that I appreciated at the time, because I was young and concentrating on enjoying myself, just what was going on behind the scenes.

I never met Arthur Hobbs, because he had retired as the first secretary of the WFA by the time that the inaugural England game was played and sadly died a few years later. Having found out about him in researching this book, I wish that he was still around so that I could thank him personally for what he did for women's football in the early days. Arthur played a leading role in the formation of the WFA in 1969 and lobbied the FA tirelessly until they rescinded their 1921 ban on women playing the game. You could say that he was highly instrumental in enabling women like myself to participate in football and get so much pleasure from the game.

Arthur's position as secretary was subsequently filled by Patricia Gregory, who had also been heavily involved in the setting up of the WFA. She was to spend many years helping to administrate the game. Patricia was one of the officials that the girls in the England team got to know very well. She was the one who wrote to us with all the details of forthcoming matches, with strict instructions on where to meet, what to bring and how we were expected to behave, paying most of the postage out of her own pocket as well as spending a fortune on the phone. Patricia often came with us on England trips to make sure that all the arrangements ran smoothly and to act as our chaperone. She had her work cut out keeping some of the younger players in order but she was pretty strict with us in the nicest possible way. She also had a wry sense of humour, which was probably just as well. On the nights before a game there was a strict curfew in place, which Patricia was always keen to enforce. On one occasion when she was out doing her rounds to make sure that everyone was in their rooms, some of the girls (I think Paddy McGroarty and Jeannie Allott might have been the main protagonists but I am not entirely sure) sneaked back to her room and put some nettles in the bottom of her bed. Patricia told me that she felt them as soon as she climbed into bed and pushed her feet downwards but there was no way that she was going to let on to the perpetrators, who she knew would be listening outside the door. She just winced quietly, removed them and carried on as if nothing had happened. That typified Patricia really, resilient, resourceful and never really fazed.

Another member of the international committee who put a phenomenal amount of work into the game was Flo Bilton, who sadly died recently. Flo was also membership secretary for the WFA for many years. She was a wonderful person who could and did turn her hand to just about anything that might help other women get enjoyment out of the game. Flo had played football herself back in the 1950s when it was really going against the grain. She ran a women's team at her workplace (Reckitt and Coleman's in Hull) and introduced Carol Thomas (née McCune) the second England captain, to the game. Flo's international duties were many and varied behind the scenes but when she wasn't meeting foreign officials at the airport, or chaperoning us at England games, Flo must have spent a lot of her spare time sewing! As the WFA had no money to fund the production of caps for the England players, Flo went ahead and made them herself. All the braiding and stitching involved must have really taken some time. Because there was no way that she could cope with the task of supplying every player with a cap for every game that they appeared in, we all just got one to mark our first appearance in the England team. At the end of our career we then received a plaque with small shields inset all the way around, recording the dates and opponents for all the subsequent games that we had played in. This is something that I know the players have all kept and treasured. Mine was actually presented to me by Flo and Carol Thomas, who turned up to surprise me with it at a sports award evening at Hull University, where I was taking a Master's degree in 1982.

It wasn't just caps that demanded Flo's sewing skills, however. She also spent a lot of time in her hotel room on one England tour fixing badges onto the England shirts that we were due to play in the next day! She had roped one of the other England officials, June Jaycocks and some the players into it as well. This might give you some idea of the sort of shoestring budget that the whole operation relied on in those days.

June Jaycocks was another good woman who was dedicated to the cause. She had played football for Brighton GPO and become chairperson of the Sussex League before becoming chair of the international committee. Her duties on England tours involved chaperoning the girls, dealing with dignitaries, smoothing things over and generally making sure everything went according to plan. I remember June as having a warm, lively personality and a great sense of humour, which made her very popular with the players. She apparently remembers me as a real joker off the pitch but a really good player on it. I think she was being tactful!

Other people that deserve a special mention are Jenny and John Bruton, who were also international officers who went away with the team; David Hunt (David was treasurer and chairman of various WFA committees) who did loads for the sport over the years and was usually at all the England home games; Ron Hyde as vice-chairman of the WFA; Gladys Aiken and Betty Gibson, who were both members of the international committee; and last but definitely not least David Marlowe, who was chairman of the WFA for a time and was involved in the administration of the organisation, in some capacity, through most of its twenty-four-year existence.

These, and others whom I probably don't know about and I apologise to if I have failed to give a mention, were some of the unsung heroes and heroines that were working on my behalf at the time that I was playing for England. It is perhaps a little late to say it now, but if you are reading this book, then thank you!

four

Media Coverage

Media coverage of women's football when I was playing in the 1970s was in the main restricted to the local and national press. There was the odd appearance of some of the England players on news/sports programmes on the television but there was no television coverage (either live or recorded) of club or England games.

Local newspaper coverage, when it appeared, was generally fine and commented on the event, the action and the results. The national (tabloid) press was another matter, however. Reporters from this type of paper seemed to have their own ideas about how they wanted to present women's football to the public. We, the players, and to a certain extent the WFA management, were fairly naïve when it came to our dealings with them in the early days. My desire to get myself into the *Daily Mail*, as this was the paper that my family read, led me to get represented in a way that was thoroughly out of character. The reporter and photographer from the *Mail* were allowed into the dressing room (never a good idea!) at Wembley stadium, where we were changing in preparation for a training session on the hallowed turf. This was just prior to setting off to Scotland for the very first England women's international match in November 1972. This, and the fact that it would be the first time that a women's international football team had set foot on the Wembley pitch, made it big news. The reporter was determined to get a picture of one of us putting on eye make-up, so that they could focus on what they always tended to do then when covering women's sport: how we looked, rather than how we played. Most of the girls sensibly refused to take part in such a ridiculous stunt but, being keen to get my picture in the paper, I volunteered. The reporter supplied the eye shadow. I certainly didn't possess any and never used it when going out for the evening, let alone when going out to play football! The whole idea was ridiculous and I have cringed many times over the years at the memory that I went along with it. My only defence is that I was young and impressionable and thought it would be great surprise for my family at the breakfast table. Sure enough, in the next day's edition of the *Mail* there was a double-page spread about us, dominated by the picture of me, accompanied by the caption 'Ready for the kick off... and Wendy Owen gives the final touch to her eye make-up.'

I may have been the one to get my photograph in the paper on that occasion but the most photographed player in that very first England squad was probably Jeannie Allott, a young attacking midfield player, who scored quite a few goals for the team. Jeannie had long blonde hair that she kept loose when playing. Apart from the obvious attraction for the press (young and blonde) Jeannie's hair appeared to be a photographer's dream because when she headed the ball her flowing locks went swirling into the air, all around her head. Numerous pictures of this nature accompanied reports on our games. One that appeared in a national tabloid was accompanied by the headline 'What a striker'. The report itself read, 'Is it a pop star? Is it a rare bird? No, it's Jeannie with the long blonde hair, showing the soccer style that bagged her a couple of goals for England.' The press were really lost for a good subject when Jeannie left England in 1976 to go to Holland to play competitive league football with ZW Rotterdam.

Typical of the frivolous nature of some of the coverage that appeared in the early 1970s was a series of photographs in the *Sun* newspaper, which, every week for a limited period, featured top players depicted as playing cards in a soccer card game. Most of the picture cards in the suit were male players but the queen was always one of the England women's team. Paddy McGroarty was pictured in a nun's habit with the caption, 'Paddy McGroarty is the queen of diamonds. She plays midfield for England Ladies. She learnt to play football while a nun.' Janet Bagguley, who was one of my friends in 'the card school', appeared as the queen of spades and was referred to as 'this charmer from Cheshire who has been called the Nobby Stiles of ladies' soccer.' It went on to remark that she, however, had all her teeth and was much better looking.

Journalists did have another aspect that they were particularly interested in other than our appearance. Favourite questions in interview were, 'Do you have a boyfriend?' and 'What does your boyfriend think about you playing football?' The 'Femail' section of the *Daily Mail* on 11 September 1973 (having obviously taken this particular tack) included the following quotes from women football players from outside the England team: 'My boyfriend has to take second place to the game', 'Soccer comes first with me', 'My husband doesn't like me playing. Typical male isn't he?'

I know that most of us in the England squad found this line of questioning very frustrating. We were serious sportswomen who wanted to be recognised in our own right, who the hell cared about what men thought? That's what we wanted to reply but we had to be a bit more diplomatic!

The amount of women's football coverage that was appearing in the tabloid press in the early 1970s probably had something to do with the game's novelty value. The fact that women's football was only just beginning to take off in England, after the lifting of the FA ban, made it newsworthy. Some papers carried articles that purported to be taking this growth seriously but in the language that they used they unfortunately missed the mark. A case in point was an article (written by Warschauer et al) that appeared in the *Sunday People* that began:

They're football crazy... they're football mad. The birds we're talking about not blokes. And we mean PLAYING not watching. It's one of the fastest-growing sports in Britain, women's football. A revolution born out of broken bra straps and muddy knickers; gone are the days when all they did was boot a ball around for a giggle. They're tough, the dolly-dribblers of Britain.

Another attempt at a serious article about the upsurge of interest in women's football appeared in the *Daily Mail* on 11/9/1973 entitled 'Why women's soccer is no longer a joke'. This starts off by offering some genuine statistics:

In two years the number of women's soccer clubs in Britain has grown from 44 to 300. This means that nearly 6,000 women are now regular team players... in 1921 the Football Association had the nerve to ban women from playing organised football, a bit of male chauvinist piggery which they replaced in 1970. Now the girls have their own Women's Football Association and their chairman, David Marlowe, claims: Women's Soccer is the international growth sport.

The article is subsequently spoilt however by its own bit of male chauvinist piggery, as it goes on to tell the reader that:

It is catching on fast in Britain but abroad it is scoring even faster. In Italy for example a woman's match can draw anything up to 7,000 spectators. Perhaps this is because Italian men like fast cars, women and football in that order and when they get women and football together the game is irresistible!

Another theme that is apparent in the early reports from the tabloid press is their tendency to want to make comparisons between men's and women's football, which is something that the FA are now keen to resist. Some of these observations were serious ones; Christine Dunn, for instance, who wrote one of the few genuinely respectful tabloid articles on the England team, which appeared in the *Daily Mail* on 19 September 1972, sought the views of the England manager on this issue. With reference to the women's game Eric

Worthington is quoted as saying: 'The big difference between this and men's football is the obvious one – the male has more strength. But apart from that there is just as much skill.'

In contrast, other contributions to the debate were, to say the least, rather flippant. A different national tabloid featured two photographs next to one another. One showed the defensive wall of the Arsenal men's team just as a free-kick was about to be taken. The other showed the England women's football team at a similar moment. In the first photo the men have their hands down low around the groin area. The women in contrast have their hands held high in front of the upper body. The header to the article reads 'Vive la difference! The hands give it away'. It goes on to comment that:

A man's instinct is to protect his manhood. You can see this graphically demonstrated in the picture on the right. A woman's instinct is clearly to protect her womanhood. The differences between men and women are evident even in such sexually neutral areas as a football field. Vive la difference!

As time went on the WFA got more streetwise to the ways of the press and were able to protect the players and give us guidance about how to avoid interview pitfalls and project a more serious image of the women's game. I found this particularly useful as I was often pushed forward by the WFA when they wanted someone to give an interview. I think that this was because I was the teacher in the squad and they thought I was more used to public speaking. As a result, I found myself summoned to a photo-call with members of the England men's team for publicity after our Home International Championship victory in May 1976. The subsequent photograph of me sandwiched between England players Gerry Francis and Mick Channon was featured in a number of papers accompanied by a serious report on our championship form.

The England press cuttings that I have kept appear to indicate that reports in the tabloids were generally becoming less frivolous as time went on. By our fifth international against Holland at Elm Park, Reading in November 1973, the focus across several newspapers is solely on the result and the football action rather than other attractions! The same is true for our eighth game against France at Wimbledon FC in November 1974, which received a lot of attention and was covered by most of the daily tabloids.

The *Daily Express* report on this game, for instance, is typical of that which appeared in three other similar papers at the same time. Entitled 'England girls are great' it goes on:

England's girls maintained their unbeaten record with a comfortable victory – their eighth in succession – at Wimbledon. England's well-drilled squad always had the beating of the talented but disunited French girls whose 4-4-2 formation could only be described as flexible. Captain Sheila Parker and sweeper Wendy Owen held the defence firm and Sandra Choate caused havoc with her tricky wing play. Pat Davies and inside-left Sue Lopez scored.

Apart from the fact that they were referring to us as 'girls' rather than 'women', that type of report was very refreshing. It was very short, however, which is true of the others in the tabloids at that time. The content was better, but the column inches devoted to women's football in that type of paper were becoming considerably shorter than they had been in 1972, when whole pages were devoted to the game. This was probably indicative of the fact that the novelty value attached to women playing football was finally wearing off.

There was a lengthier and far more detailed report of the action in that same France game, however, that was written by Richard Yallop of the *Guardian*. In it he notes that Don Revie (who was manager of the England men's team at the time) and Ted Croker (secretary of the FA) had sent best wishes to our team by telegram. This again appears to suggest that the England women's football team was being taken far more seriously in various quarters by 1974. I have several of Richard Yallop's pieces in my collection, which are the only examples that I have of broadsheet coverage from that time. That is not to say that the *Guardian* was the only broadsheet newspaper that was covering our games. I am sure that there would have been others.

Overall, however, despite the flurry of media attention that the game received at the very beginning, as time went on women's football settled into the position that it continues to hold, that of a low-profile sport, a poor relation in comparison to the men's game.

The situation is improving; media coverage of women's football has increased considerably in recent years, to include regular weekly reports in the tabloids and the broadsheets, as well as live television coverage of events like the FA Women's Cup final, the Olympics and the World Cup. The coverage is deadly serious and treats its subject with respect. This was something that was a rare commodity in our encounters with the press as members of the first England women's football team.

five

Off to the USA

One of the spin-offs of being an England international player was having the opportunity to travel to the USA to coach at various soccer camps during the 1970s. Women's soccer was in its infancy in the USA at that time. It was beginning in schools and camps but collegiate and national team soccer was yet to take off. At the time no one could have predicted that by 2004 the USA women would have won two World Cups and two Olympic gold medals.

Because the game had yet to develop over there, there was a dearth of top-class female players and coaches in the country and they had to look further afield to fill coaching positions. Women's football in England was hardly far advanced, particularly on the coaching side (the first Preliminary Coaching Certificate course for women did not take place until August 1974), but compared to the USA it was streets ahead. There was a recognised governing body, a competitive league structure, a national cup competition and a national team.

Fortunately, therefore, when soccer organisers from the USA came calling, I was in the right place at the right time, with the best credentials that were available. I was playing for England, training to be a PE teacher and about to become one of the first female Preliminary Licence football coaches in this country.

HARTWICK COLLEGE, ONEONTA, 1974

In the spring of 1974, while I was in my second year at Dartford College, I was contacted out of the blue by Roley Howard, the manager of Marine Football Club in Southport. He asked me if I would like to join a group of coaches from the Southport Coaching Association, who were going out to the USA that summer to staff a soccer camp at Hartwick College, in Oneonta, New York State. Roley was co-ordinating things over in England, for the camp's organiser, Francisco Marcos.

Marcos was one of US soccer's visionary pioneers. A graduate of Hartwick College, he was to go on to make a massive contribution to the development of soccer in America over the next thirty years. He was to spend ten years, from 1974 onwards, working at a high level for various professional clubs in the NASL (North American Soccer League) and then became the founder and commissioner of America's largest group of professional and amateur soccer leagues (United Soccer Leagues).

In his plans for summer 1974, he was already demonstrating his eye for the trailblazing idea and had decided that as there were already a lot of soccer camps in the US, he would do something at Hartwick that was that bit different from the rest. He would run an international youth tournament and a camp alongside one another, bring in coaches from overseas and attempt to hire an international female soccer player/coach as a role model to sell the camp to girls as well as boys. In order to achieve the last of these objectives Francisco had contacted the WFA in England to see if they could recommend anyone. They had given him my details.

When Roley Howard phoned me on Francisco's behalf I was very excited by the whole idea. I was being offered three weeks' coaching experience in the USA, with air fares paid for and living expenses provided for the duration of the stay. For a fledgling football coach and a penniless student teacher this was a very attractive proposition. I was quite apprehensive, however, at the thought of going so far away from home, with people that I didn't know. The fact that I would be the only female coach, both in the travelling party and at the camp itself, was also a fairly daunting prospect for a twenty-year-old.

I didn't make a decision straight away but asked for time to think things over. In the meantime I discussed the offer with my parents and the WFA. Everyone was very encouraging and supportive of my ability to make a success of the trip. This helped to give me the courage to grasp an opportunity which was, after all, far too good to miss.

I flew out to the USA in July 1974 after my college had broken up for the summer vacation. I met up with the Southport group, in London, at the airport. The other coaches in the party were Roley Howard, Ken Spencer, Alan Spence and John Armstrong. I can remember feeling very apprehensive on the flight over and it wasn't just my fear of flying that was worrying me. My first impression was that everyone else seemed to be far more qualified and experienced than me. Roley, Ken and John were all FA Preliminary Badge coaches. Alan Spence had his full badge and was a course tutor for the FA. Roley Howard had been managing Marine Football Club in the Cheshire League since 1972 and prior to that had managed the second team at Formby. Incidentally, in researching this book, I discovered that, thirty-three years on, Roley has only just retired from managing Marine FC, who are now in the

Unibond Northern Premier League. This made him the longest-serving football manager in Great Britain.

Even though I had been head-hunted and was probably one of the best females that Francisco Marcos could find at that time, in comparison to the male coaches I felt rather short on experience and training. My football coaching background was hardly extensive at this point. I had performed the role of player/coach to the Dartford College women's team in the 1973/74 season (a team that I had established when it had become too difficult to travel home at weekends to play for Thame). Apart from that, most of my experience was as a player. I wasn't due to take my WFA Preliminary Coaching Certificate at Lilleshall until after I returned from the USA that August. I did, however, have a good understanding of how to organise and teach sporting activities and some school teaching experience under my belt. This was a product of my ongoing PE teacher-training course at Dartford College, which had a reputation for producing excellent teachers. I had also had the benefit of seeing some top-class FA staff coaches at work at England training sessions. This was to stand me in good stead during the coming weeks.

After a fairly smooth flight we landed in New York. This was my first time on US soil and I was full of excitement and anticipation. We were met at the airport by Francisco, who was to drive us on the very long journey to Oneonta, which is in upstate New York, nearly into Canada. On the first part of the journey we went right through the centre of New York at night with all the lights ablaze. This was my first and only sight of the city on that trip and it made a big impression on me. I was craning my neck out of the window, trying to look up towards the tops of the buildings that were towering above us on all sides. I would have loved to have stopped and got out but we whizzed straight through as we had a long way to go.

After driving for what seemed like forever, we finally arrived at Hartwick College, which was to be our home for the next three weeks. We were staying in the student accommodation and I don't think that I have ever been so grateful to arrive at my destination and fall into bed.

The next day we had the chance to relax a bit and explore our surroundings before meeting up with the other coaches to find out about the schedule for the coming weeks. The Hartwick College campus was in a lovely setting. It was not far from the Canadian border (only about an hour or two from Niagara Falls) with the hills making a beautiful backdrop in the near distance. The college had impressive sports facilities and the nearby town of Oneonta had all the necessary amenities (two bars, a hamburger joint and a doughnut house!) without being too large and intimidating. It was a perfect setting for me on my first trip to the country.

The camp was being held shortly after the 1974 Men's World Cup, to take best advantage of the publicity that this had given to soccer in the US. It was organised around an international youth tournament, which involved sixteen teams of under-sixteen and under-nineteen-year-old boys from seven different countries. They all stayed on the campus and played matches in the afternoons. In the mornings there was a coaching programme for local children, which was staffed by both English and US-based coaches. This was what I was to be involved in.

In addition to the group over from England, there was a strong contingent of coaches drawn from the Hartwick College men's team. These included players from overseas as well as homegrown talent from the USA. Hartwick was a powerhouse for men's soccer in the US at that time. It was one of the first colleges to bring players over from England, among other countries, on scholarships, which meant that they were being funded to study at the college while playing for the soccer team. In recent years, following the huge growth and success of the women's game in the USA, this kind of opportunity has opened up for female soccer players, but it was not available at the time as college soccer for women was only being played at a very minor level.

As the only female coach at camp, I was responsible for the delivery of the programme for the girls who had signed up. As far as I can remember, the group size each week was fairly small (twelve to fifteen players at the most), which again reflected the fact that at that time, girls' and women's football in the USA was only in the very early stages of development.

Coaching sessions at the camp were held every morning (for about four hours) for the whole week. In the afternoons I was free to either watch the tournament matches or do my own thing. As a fairly inexperienced coach, initially I found it a struggle to think of enough material to keep the same group of girls involved and interested for a whole week. Consequently, I spent most of my afternoons devising practices and games for the next day. I remember utilising drills that I had participated in myself at England training sessions and endeavouring to adapt them for younger players. This was all a bit hit and miss I'm sure, but the girls seemed to enjoy themselves and improved greatly by the end of the week.

I discovered very early on that English was not quite the universal language that I thought it was. There were several terms that I had to quickly get to grips with to make myself understood as an English coach working in the USA. One of these was the word 'scrimmage', which means a competitive game of soccer. Another was 'soccer cleats', which are football boots. Finally, when you wanted the children to put training bibs on, you had to ask them to 'go and put on a pinnie'. If you forgot and used the English terms the players had no idea what you were talking about!

During the first week I was very homesick, probably due to the fact that I was young, the only female coach and thousands of miles away from home. Another contributory factor was the amount of free time that I had, most of which I was spending on my own. Anyone who has experienced homesickness will know how dreadful and debilitating the feeling can be. Fortunately, Francisco Marcos was very sympathetic towards me and helped me through the problem.

By the second week I was feeling much better. By then I had got to know some of the other coaches and begun to enjoy their company in the evenings. We often went out to the local bar in Oneonta and then on to the coffee house, where we ate doughnuts, drank coffee and chatted into the small hours. This proved to be quite a tiring schedule but I was young and still able to be up bright and early the next morning ready to deliver my coaching sessions!

Funnily enough, one evening it came up in conversation that one of the other English coaches, Farrukh Quraishi, had played in a boys' football team in Slough that my father had managed. He credited my Dad with providing him with one of his earliest opportunities to become involved in and enjoy the game. Farrukh had been brought over to the US by Francisco Marcos to play collegiate soccer at Oneonta State, where Francisco was assistant recruiter and assistant coach. He was to go on to play professional soccer in the North American Soccer League for the Tampa Bay Rowdies. This was an amazing coincidence that made me realise what a small world it really is. It also somehow made me feel that bit closer to home.

My confidence in my coaching ability began to grow as the weeks went by. The sessions that I had planned were being well received and the girls were outgoing, precocious and great fun to work with. Hopefully I provided them with the type of positive female role model that I had been hired to portray, one that had not been available to me when I started to play the game in England in the 1960s. Francisco Marcos has recently told me that he marketed the camp to the girls on the fact that an England international female player was going to be there. Even though he hadn't seen me coach and was only going on recommendation, he brought me out because he felt that the important thing was to be pioneering. It was to be one of the first (if not the first) camps to have a good woman player that the girls could identify with, to show that a woman could play and coach and that this was something that they really could aspire to.

By the end of the camp I was loving every minute of being in the USA. I liked the food, which was plentiful and very different to what I was used to, waffles and maple syrup, hamburgers and cream-filled doughnuts having yet to cross the Atlantic. I loved the fact that you could stay out until three or four in the morning in a relatively small town and still find a restaurant or coffee bar that was open. The kids were great, the weather was glorious and it was wonderful to be among a group of male soccer coaches who respected my ability and knowledge of the game and treated me as an equal. What was really noticeable to me, particularly with the US coaches and their attitude towards me and the girls at the camp, was that no one seemed to have any problem with the idea of girls and women playing soccer. It did not appear to be regarded primarily as a man's game. This was very different to my experiences back home in England.

After camp was over, as our return tickets had been left open, I elected to stay on for an extra week rather than travel straight home with the others. One of the US coaches had invited me back to his home to stay with his family and I was keen to experience ordinary life over there. Unfortunately I can't remember all the details of this (such as who I stayed with and where) but what does stick in my mind is the warmth and great hospitality that was shown towards me. I was treated like a celebrity. On one occasion a party was thrown in my honour because their family and friends were dying to meet me. Everyone seemed to be really interested to hear about England and loved my accent. People would come over to me and ask me to say something, anything, just so that they could hear me talk!

When I returned home to my own family I was full of enthusiastic stories about my adventures. I was also proud of what I had achieved. I had overcome my anxieties to travel all that way as the lone female and had made a success of my coaching when I got there. I liked what I had seen of the country and the culture (especially the very positive attitude towards female soccer players and coaches) and was determined to try to return to the USA again, as soon as the opportunity presented itself.

TAMPA BAY ROWDIES, TAMPA, FLORIDA: 1978

I had to wait four years for this to happen and once again I received the invitation via an unexpected phone call from a complete stranger. I did know the caller by reputation, however. Gordon Hill had been a top-flight English Football League referee in the 1960s and early 1970s. His face became a very familiar one on our television screens. A headmaster in his day job, he had commanded great respect from the players and regularly officiated in matches at the highest level. Gordon was ringing me from Tampa, in Florida, with a dream invitation to go out to the sunshine coast for six weeks in the summer of 1978 to coach for the Tampa Bay Rowdies, one of the top clubs in the professional men's North American Soccer League (NASL). I couldn't believe my ears.

As the conversation progressed I discovered that Francisco Marcos was once again behind the offer. He had moved to Tampa late in 1974 to take up a new appointment as the director of public relations/community relations and development at the club. Francisco was in at the very start of things, being the second person to be appointed by the club's millionaire owner George Strawbridge Junior. The Rowdies had found almost instant success by winning the Soccer Bowl in 1975. This meant that they were overall champions of the NASL for that season.

Gordon Hill was brought out to Tampa in 1976, after he had retired from teaching, as director of youth development. Part of his role was to co-ordinate Kamp Kick in the Grass, which was the name given to the Rowdies' youth soccer camp programme. When he was looking for a female coach to work with the girls at the summer camps, Francisco suggested me. Although there had been some growth in participation in girls' and women's soccer in the US since 1974 there was still no national team. Top women player/coaches were still therefore something of a rarity and the idea of bringing over an England women's international player to boost female interest in the game and the club was again seen as a smart marketing move.

This time I didn't hesitate and ask for time to consider the offer. I jumped at the chance to go back over to the States to work for such a prestigious club. The Tampa Bay Rowdies were well known in England. Rodney Marsh of Fulham, QPR, Manchester City and England, a very talented player and a flamboyant character, had made a high-profile exit from Manchester City to go over to play for them in 1976. He was one of many British stars, many of whom were past masters, who were at that time joining the exodus to the USA to play pro-league soccer. George Best had been over there since 1974, playing first for the Los Angeles Aztecs and then joining Gordon Banks at Fort Lauderdale Strikers. Bobby Moore and Geoff Hurst went out in 1976 to play for San Antonio Thunder and Seattle Sounders respectively. The comedian Jasper Carrott had raised the British public's awareness of both the Rowdies and the NASL by going over to Florida to make a television documentary about them that I, along with many others, had watched. Consequently, when I told people where I was going they all seemed to have heard about Rodney Marsh's Tampa Bay Rowdies and were suitably impressed.

The local press, both in the Medway Towns area of Kent, where I was teaching PE in a local secondary school, and back in my home town of Beaconsfield, soon got wind of the story. 'Wendy flies out to join the Rowdies', 'Wendy to coach USA soccer girls', 'Teacher signs for Florida football team' and 'Wendy joins soccer exodus to America' appeared as headlines to the stories that were written about my forthcoming trip. Photographers came to take pictures of me at the school where I was teaching, the Hundred of Hoo School, near Rochester, which caused quite a stir of excitement among the pupils, particularly the under-fifteen boys' football team that I had been coaching for several years. I think that they were secretly quite proud of their teacher and coach.

Press interest was not restricted to this side of the water. The Rowdies were keen to publicise my impending arrival and had alerted journalists in Tampa. Several weeks before I was due to set off, I did a transatlantic telephone interview for a magazine from the Bay area that resulted in the appearance of a full-page article, with accompanying photograph, entitled 'Camp Kikinthagrass: Female International Soccer Player to instruct Girls'. The journalist (Michelle Jones) went on to comment that: 'Her example will undoubtedly be the first exposure these girls will have to a female that can do everything that male soccer players can. The experience should instil confidence and pride.' As I prepared to fly out to the States in mid-July, I hoped that I could live up to my billing!

I was going to spend the first two weeks of my visit coaching at one of the Rowdies' satellite camps at Belmont Abbey College in Charlotte, North Carolina. After that, I was due to travel back down to spend a month in Tampa. On this trip to the USA I would be travelling solo. The journey involved a long flight from Heathrow to Miami. In Miami I had to change planes and fly the short hop to Tampa, where I would be met by Gordon Hill. After an overnight stay in Tampa, I was due to fly on the next morning to North Carolina via Atlanta. This itinerary was going to involve a total of four take-offs and landings. This was pretty daunting for someone with a real fear of flying!

Although I was apprehensive about the flying, I was far more confident this time about my ability to do the coaching job once I arrived. Four years on and I was far more qualified and experienced than I had been for the Oneonta trip. I had gained my Preliminary Coaching Certificate in August 1974, after attending the first course for women at Lilleshall National Sports Centre. This was organised by the WFA and staffed by Tommy Tranter, who was the England women's team manager and an FA staff coach. Five people from the course had passed (the others were Carol McCune and Sue Lopez, who were both colleagues of mine from the England team, Jane Talbot, our England team physiotherapist, and Pauline Dickie from Southampton Ladies FC). We became the first qualified female football coaches in the country.

Since qualifying I had also gained a lot more coaching experience. My player/manager role with the Dartford College women had continued and I had steered the team to a quarter-final place in the WFA Cup in the 1976/77 season. I had also coached the Kent Women's League representative team.

By that summer of 1978 I was a qualified PE teacher with three years of secondary school teaching experience under my belt. When the school had not been willing to allow me to start a girls' football team I had turned to coaching the boys, leading the same group of lads to some notable successes in inter-school competitions from under-thirteen through to under-fifteen age level.

Consequently, given my achievements since my last trip to the US, as I sat on the plane to Florida contemplating the challenges that I might have to face over the next six weeks, I felt in a much better position to rise to meet them.

Luckily the journey went pretty smoothly. There were no dramas on either of the flights or on the changeover at Miami airport. I managed to arrive on time, with my luggage, to meet Gordon Hill in Tampa. Gordon was instantly recognisable. He was tall, thin and still athletic-looking. Apart from being a little older and sporting a Florida suntan, he had changed little from his refereeing days. After greeting me warmly he loaded my luggage into the back of his waiting car and drove me to my hotel. The club were funding an overnight stay in a really plush hotel so that I could relax properly before flying to North Carolina the next day. Gordon left me there, promising to return the next morning to take me back to the airport, with instructions to order anything that I liked via room service and to put it on the bill.

After such a long and exhausting journey it was wonderful to be staying in such luxurious surroundings. The hotel room had two double beds, an en-suite bathroom, which was not something that was standard in hotels in England at that time, and a balcony overlooking the swimming pool and the bay. It was absolutely fantastic. Taking Gordon at his word, I surveyed the room service menu and felt very decadent when a waiter delivered an enormous club sandwich and drinks to my door. The whole hotel experience was totally new for me and made me feel very pampered and special. After eating, watching some American TV and making my choice from the two enormous and very comfortable double beds, I fell asleep, totally exhausted.

I did just about manage to wake up and be ready the next morning when Gordon came to pick me up. My journey that day was in two stages. Firstly, I had to fly from Tampa to Atlanta and then on from there to North Carolina. Although Gordon was going to put me on the plane at Tampa, I would be making the trip on my own. I was anxious from the outset because the plane that I was travelling on was very small, seating no more than about thirty people. This reminded me of the awful flight back from France with Thame Ladies FC back in 1972. Take-off from Tampa was relatively smooth, but we hadn't been airborne for very long when, without warning, the plane suddenly dropped like a stone for a distance of about thirty or forty feet before levelling off. I was absolutely terrified and let out a gasp in fright. I thought that we were going into a crash dive. The man sitting next to me was obviously aware of my distress and kindly explained to me that in Florida the warm air caused lots of thermal currents that made it fairly commonplace for a plane to drop in that manner. I wished that someone had warned me beforehand as I was now in a state of shock that lasted for the rest of the journey! I was more than relieved to arrive at my destination (Charlotte, North Carolina) in one piece.

My home for the next two weeks was to be Belmont Abbey College in Belmont, which was just a few miles outside Charlotte. This was a higher education college set in beautiful surroundings with an abbey and a Benedictine monastery within its sprawling grounds. As it was the summer vacation we were to stay in the student accommodation, take our meals in the college refectory and make use of the college's grass soccer pitches as well as other sports facilities on the campus. I was very pleased to find myself living and working in such a lovely place.

Once again I was going to be the only female coach at the camp. There were, however, far more girls on the camp this time around than there had been at Hartwick College in 1974. I soon discovered that this wasn't going to be a problem. Everyone was very friendly and supportive and as a group we (the coaches) mixed in together and had a great time both on and off the field. The children were fun to work with and I really felt far more confident in my ability to deliver good sessions for them this time around than I had on my last trip to the USA back in 1974.

At some point in each of the weeks at camp a couple of the Tampa Bay Rowdies players would fly in, work for an afternoon with the kids and sign autographs for them. This was all part and parcel of the Rowdies' Kamp Kick in the Grass programme, which was designed not only to develop the children's skills but also to promote both the game of soccer and the club.

After the two weeks at camp in North Carolina, I flew back down to Tampa with some of the other coaches. Gordon Hill and his family generously welcomed me into their home in nearby Clearwater, which was a beautiful coastal town with an endless white sandy beach leading down to the blue warm waters of the Gulf of Mexico. I was very fortunate to be invited to stay with them for a whole month. During that time I would be able to undertake some coaching work with women's teams in the Tampa Bay area, go to some Rowdies games and have some time off to go to the beach and visit some of Florida's famous tourist attractions.

What struck me immediately on arriving back in Tampa was the stifling humidity. The weather in Florida was very different to that in North Carolina, where it had been hot but bearable. August in Tampa is the hurricane season. The sun shines relentlessly by day, with temperatures reaching well above 30°c and humidity up to around ninety-eight per cent. At night you can usually expect a spectacular tropical storm, with Tampa living up to its reputation as 'the lightning capital of the world.' The only way to survive as an unacclimatised Brit is to either do very little until the sun goes down, or move smartly between air-conditioned buildings and an air-conditioned car. I did a bit of both. As it was too hot for me to coach soccer in the day, I arranged evening coaching sessions with local women's teams. During the daytime, I either relaxed at the house or beach or travelled into Tampa with Gordon to the office, or to promotional events to gain an insight into the running of the Tampa Bay Rowdies soccer club.

The club, like all the others in the NASL, was in the business of trying to sell the game of soccer to a community that was obsessed with homegrown sports such as American Football and baseball. Soccer had been around for a long time, brought over to the US by various immigrant ethnic groups, but getting it accepted by the nation as a whole had been an uphill struggle. Soccer tended, perhaps, to be regarded as a slightly effeminate game, not one that was played by 'real men'. The absence of a male identity for the sport was something that probably helped the women's game to develop and ultimately outstrip the men's in terms of success and popularity in the USA.

The Tampa Bay Rowdies went about the task of converting the American public to soccer by firstly trying to ensure that they had an entertaining, quality product. They didn't, as yet, have any depth of homegrown talent so, in common with other NASL clubs, they imported players from abroad. The Rowdies' team was mostly made up of Brits with a few US-born players to ensure that they met the required quota of fielding at least two in every game. In 1978 they also had a British manager, Gordon Jago, who had previously managed at both Millwall and QPR. All the top clubs also felt that they needed at least one star to pull in the crowds. The New York Cosmos had Pele, the LA Strikers had George Best and so in 1976 the Tampa Bay Rowdies had signed Rodney Marsh. He was their first big name and he had a flamboyant personality to match his style of play. The crowds loved him and flocked to see him. According to Francisco Marcos, at an early press conference Rodney had been asked how playing soccer in the US compared to playing in England. He had replied, 'football in England is a grey game, played on grey days, by grey people', whereas he was now in Florida, in the sunshine, having a great time.

Having a quality product was the first step, but the club then needed to ensure that the public bought into it. They attempted to do this by implementing a community relations programme aimed at encouraging people to play the game and come out to watch the Rowdies' team in action. It involved player-development work through camps and clinics, the setting up of local leagues to promote participation and the staging of regular guest appearances by the Rowdies' players and coaches in the community to make the fans feel a sense of belonging to the club. Developing and overseeing this programme was a large part of Francisco Marcos' brief. According to Francisco it was aimed at the whole community, all ages and sexes, and was very successful. 'Entire families came out to watch matches, went to clinics and signed up for leagues.' He estimated that girls and women became thirty per cent of the Rowdies' audience as they stole them away from American Football.

The coaching that I was doing for the Rowdies that summer was all part and parcel of this programme. I had already worked with the girls at Kamp Kick in the Grass in North Carolina. Now that I was back in Tampa, the club offered my services to teams in the local women's league that they had been instrumental in setting up. There was a good response, with clubs jumping at the chance to get some free coaching from a female England international soccer player. I was kept busy for most of August, working with players of varying standards throughout the Bay Area and was well received wherever I went.

As well as experiencing my coaching, the players were keen to talk to me about women's soccer in England and my international adventures. Consequently, I was invariably invited back for a post-session drink with the team at the local bar. This led to various social invitations and offers to show me around Florida's tourist attractions, such as Busch Gardens and Disney World. Once again I was overwhelmed by the warmth and hospitality shown towards me by the American people. I made friendships with women soccer players on that trip that were to last for the next twenty years.

In addition to being involved in camps and coaching clinics I also got the chance to observe some of the Rowdies' other promotional activities. I attended several events in Tampa, where the players met with either the press or the public, to answer questions about the team's performances or other aspects concerning the club. What struck me was how accessible the players were to their community compared to back home in England. Putting in these appearances was considered to be an important part of the job, particularly after home matches when players joined the fans in bar/restaurants such as Victoria Station, Fanny's and Friday's and mingled freely among them.

Francisco Marcos told me that Rodney Marsh could be totally unpredictable when it came to trying to get him to turn up to press conferences, dressed in suitable attire. Apparently on one occasion Francisco had particularly impressed upon him the importance of looking smart as he would be fronting the show. He duly turned up in his best three-piece Carnaby Street suit, but barefoot. When Francisco gave him a questioning look, Rodney said, 'you said dressed up, but you didn't say anything about shoes!' This incident probably says something about Rodney Marsh's reported sense of humour and desire to surprise people.

At one of the press conferences that I attended I was flattered to be approached by a journalist from one of the local papers, who wanted to interview me. Paul Roach, staff writer for the *St Petersburg Times* was keen to write a piece with a comparative angle and wanted to elicit my perceptions on the differences between women's soccer in England and the USA at that moment in time. Twenty-five years on, the views that I expressed for that article make interesting reading. Asked about attitudes towards women playing the sport, I tell the reporter that, in England, the prevailing view is that men are better at soccer than women and for women to play is unladylike. My observation on the situation in the US is that women playing soccer is not seen as unfeminine, so the game has a much better chance of getting off the ground and being allowed to develop alongside the men's game.

I go on to talk about low levels of involvement, lack of funding and poor publicity for women's soccer in England and the problems of gaining access to qualified coaching. My perception is that there is a greater emphasis on sport in general in the US, which should benefit the future development of women's soccer. I suggest that young girls starting out in the game in the US are already at a comparative advantage as they appear to have earlier access to sound coaching advice than their English counterparts.

Looking back on these comments now, I am sure that most of them would not be out of place in a contemporary discussion of the reasons why women's soccer in the USA, after a much later start, has far outstripped the women's game in England, both in terms of participation levels and success in international competition. Perhaps the most crucial issue to bring to this debate, however, is one raised by the article's author (Paul Roach), namely the influence of equal opportunities legislation on the provision and funding of women's sports.

By that summer of 1978 the impact of Title 1X of the Educational Amendments of 1972 was finally beginning to be felt in the USA. This piece of legislation was directed towards achieving gender equality in education and made equal access and equal spending on athletics programmes in schools and colleges mandatory. According to Francisco Marcos, it took five to ten years from the time that this legislation was passed for it to have a real effect. Women's soccer was therefore taking off at just the right time to take advantage of this. Schools and colleges throughout the country were beginning to introduce girls' and women's soccer programmes to match those that were already in place for males. In NASL-franchised cities, those schools that needed help were turning to their professional club and asking them to come in to run coaching clinics and give advice. Title 1X was to give the sport a real boost in terms of provision and funding, which propelled it forward.

Unfortunately there was no equivalent process going on in England at that time. Schools and colleges were not obliged to put football on the curricular or extracurricular programme for girls just because it was available to boys. The school that I was teaching in actively discouraged me from setting up a girls' team, which was why I ended up coaching the boys. Getting girls'/women's football into the education system was therefore proving to be an uphill battle. The Sex Discrimination Act of 1975 also had little impact on provision for women's sport in England because, crucially, it made private clubs exempt from its provisions. Ironically, this was precisely where most of the sport in England was taking place.

Differences in the scope and impact of equal opportunities legislation in the 1970s was, therefore, another possible reason why women's football in England soon fell behind while the game in the USA forged ahead.

My visit to Florida had so far given me a tantalising glimpse into a con-trasting sporting world, but my greatest insight into the cultural differences between soccer in the USA and England was gained when I attended my first Tampa Bay Rowdies match! I soon discovered that 'going to the game' in the US wasn't just about watching the soccer; it was a total family entertainment package. In Tampa, this began two hours before kick-off with a 'cook-out' in the giant car park surrounding the out-of-town stadium. I could hardly believe my eyes as families drew up in their cars, opened the boot, set-up the barbecue and began cooking steaks and burgers. This was not something that I had ever experienced as a Fulham supporter! After tucking into this fare and packing everything away it was time to go into the ground where more surprises were in store. The Buccaneer Stadium was absolutely massive. It was so called because it was, first and foremost, home to the American Football team the Tampa Bay Buccaneers. The Rowdies shared it with them. A wide tunnel walkway ran right around the inside of the ground, underneath the seating area, a bit like in the old Wembley Stadium. The similarities ended there how-ever. Instead of being home to the odd hot-dog stall and tea bar, the whole area contained a wide array of entertainment choices catering for those members of the family who had no interest in watching the soccer. There were bars and restaurants where anyone who hadn't participated in the barbecue, or was still peckish, could relax and have a drink or a decent meal. Walking further around I discovered a disco for young people, which was already in full swing. Just along from this there was an audience listening to the performance of a live band. This was definitely nothing like a trip to Craven Cottage!

When we finally made it to our seats, looking around, I was immediately struck by the difference in the composition of the crowd. In my experience of spectating at football matches in England in the 1960s and early 1970s, girls and women had been very much in the minority. Here there were men, women and children of all ages. It was definitely a family affair.

Before the game got underway there was more entertainment on the pitch from the cheerleaders, cuddly mascots and, if my memory serves me correctly, someone parachuting down into the ground. None of this razzmatazz had yet been witnessed in England. By the time the teams came out to play I was already exhausted! I was looking forward to everyone settling down so that I could relax and watch the match.

The game kicked off and I waited and waited but the crowd didn't settle down. I soon realised that the Americans have a totally different way of watch-ing soccer to the Brits. They don't actually fully concentrate. They chat, get up and walk about, go down in the middle of the play to get a hamburger or beer and buy popcorn and coke from vendors who wander up and down the ter-races and along the rows. All of this happens during the soccer action! I found this extremely annoying and distracting at first. I had to bite my tongue, as I wanted to tell people to sit down, shut up and watch the game. I did get more used to it after I had been to a few matches but basically, coming from England, I found this whole concept of sports spectating totally alien.

Another thing that was different about soccer in the US was the rules. In order to make the game more exciting as a spectacle to sell to the American public, the NASL had made certain changes to the laws of the game. FIFA were never entirely happy about this, but let them go ahead, solely for matches played in the US domestic league. The NASL organisers wanted plenty of goal-mouth action and a result every time. They didn't want the public leaving the ground disappointed, after a boring 0-0 draw!

In order to try to achieve these objectives, they changed the offside rule, introducing an offside line thirty-five yards out and stipulated that there was to be a period of extra time, followed if necessary by a penalty shoot-out, to decide all games that ended at full-time in a draw. This did seem to have the desired effect. In matches that I saw, the thirty-five-yard offside line gave midfield players more space to work in, in order to set up attacks, while players like Rodney Marsh had a field day up front. Having also witnessed the tension and excitement of the penalty shoot-out in the semi-final of the 1978 Soccer Bowl at Tampa Stadium, I have to admit that the 'American rules' had a lot going for them.

The Rowdies' opponents in that semi-final were George Best's Fort Lauderdale Strikers (he had joined them in June, from the LA Aztecs). So here I was, all the way out in Florida, watching George Best play against Rodney Marsh. This was pretty coincidental, because the last time that I had seen them together was during the 1976/77 English Football League season, when they both played for Fulham, the team that I had supported since childhood. They were able to do this because the seasons in the US and England did not coincide and they had an agreement with their clubs.

The semi-final was a two-legged affair. The first leg had been won by Fort Lauderdale on their home turf. Now the Rowdies had them back at Tampa for the return match, with a coveted place in the Soccer Bowl final at stake. I watched the game from the lofty heights of the press box, which was perched way up on the top of the stadium. I had been given a VIP press pass for the occasion. It was a fantastic experience to see what went on up there. I got to see and hear the commentators in action. It was so high up, however, that the players were quite small figures in the distance and I was divorced, to a certain extent, from the excitement of the crowd.

Nevertheless, it was an absolutely gripping match. It had everything: a big storm, which left the pitch covered in water; overtime, because the Rowdies had won the match in normal time to square the tie; then, when extra time had finished goal-less, we were into the penalty shoot-out situation.

The NASL rules for a shoot-out were very different to FIFA's. This was another aspect that had been changed to make things more exciting for the crowd. Instead of taking a normal kick from the penalty spot, the attacker started with the ball on the thirty-five-yard line, then, on the referee's signal, had five seconds to run towards the goal and attempt to score. The goalkeeper was allowed to come out and close down the attacker to try and stop him from scoring, using any means within the rules governing what a 'keeper was allowed to do in normal play.

There was always the potential for great drama in this method of deciding a match and, as the first penalty taker for Fort Lauderdale stepped up to the line, the crowd was holding its breath, waiting to see what would unfold. The whistle went and he set off, but was unlucky enough to get the ball stuck in one of the many puddles that the storm had left on the playing surface. By the time that he had extricated it, the goalkeeper had come right out and smothered the shot. Fort Lauderdale now needed the Rowdies to miss one. We were biting our nails in the press box, willing the team home. It was level pegging when Rodney Marsh, the captain, came forward to take the final crucial penalty. He just needed to score and it would be all over. Despite the difficult conditions Rodney held his nerve. As the ball hit the back of the net, the home fans erupted. For the second time in their short history, the Tampa Rowdies were through to the final of the Soccer Bowl.

Sadly, I would not be around to witness their exploits in that match as my Florida adventure was drawing to a close. The drama and excitement of that semi-final night would, however, be one of the great memories that I would take home with me. Others would include the warmth and hospitality shown towards me by everyone that I had come into contact with; the skill and enthusiasm shown by the girls and women that I had worked with and the respect that had once again been afforded to me as a female player and coach.

The Tampa Bay Rowdies had been excellent hosts and a great club to work for. They had given me an exciting opportunity to travel, coach soccer and gain an insight into the workings of a top professional men's team at a high point in the history of the NASL. As I said goodbye to Gordon Hill and his family and prepared to fly home, my main hope was that I could return the next year, perhaps for more than just the summer. After all that I had seen of girls' and women's soccer in the USA, over the six weeks, I had a strong hunch that the game was set to take off and go places and I was eager to try to return to play a part in it.

As a postscript, the reader might be interested to know how the Rowdies got on in that 1978 Soccer Bowl Final. After following the team all summer, when I arrived home in England, I was keen to find out myself. Their opponents were the mighty New York Cosmos, the winners of the 1977 Soccer Bowl. This was the team that Pele had joined in 1975. His last game for them had been in the previous year's final against the Seattle Sounders. Although Pele would not be playing for them this time, they had other international forwards (such as Italy's Giorgio Chinaglia and England's Dennis Tueart) to fall back on. Backed by Warner Brothers, the Cosmos were the wealthiest and most powerful club in the NASL and, going into the game, were the strong favourites to retain their title.

Sadly it was not to be the fairytale ending to the Tampa Bay Rowdies' season that everyone connected with the club, including myself, had hoped for. This time there had been no heroics from Rodney Marsh because he had pulled out of the game through injury. Without his skill and firepower up front the Rowdies found themselves wanting and were, in the end, beaten quite easily 3-1. It had still been a great season, however, by any standards, and there was always the next one to look forward to.

THE SOCCER FARM, POMFRET, CONNECTICUT, 1979

I did go back out to the USA the following summer but not to work for the Rowdies as planned. Everything had been set up for this to happen but at the last minute things had gone awry. Gordon Hill had contacted me again in the spring of 1979 to ask me if I would come over to coach for the summer at two of the Rowdies' satellite camps. I was to spend two weeks in Denver, Colorado and then move on to New Orleans. These were two fantastic places that I was dying to visit, so I was absolutely thrilled to get such a wonderful assignment. I was also really looking forward to working for the Rowdies again as they had treated me so well the previous year.

I was all set to go when, a couple of months before I was due to fly out, I had a call from Gordon Hill with some bad news. For some reason, perhaps because the venues were so far away from Tampa, the camps in Denver and New Orleans had failed to recruit enough children and were being pulled from the schedule. As all the other camps were now fully staffed there was no job for me that summer after all. Gordon was extremely apologetic but I was absolutely devastated. It had been a dream ticket and all of a sudden it was being taken away from me.

There was nothing for it but to attempt to make other last-minute arrangements to save my summer from becoming a complete disaster. I thought that I might go back to work for the Rowdies the following year but, as I had by then made other contacts, it never happened.

I did follow the fortunes of the Rowdies over the subsequent years however. Rodney Marsh got his chance to play in a Soccer Bowl final in the summer of 1979, as the club continued where it had left off the year before. Unfortunately the team was on the losing end of things again, beaten this time by the Vancouver

Whitecaps. This was to be Marsh's last game for the club as a player. He was brought back in 1984, as coach, but by then the NASL, and the Rowdies, had gone into an irreversible decline. The league eventually folded in 1985.

In researching this book I spoke to Rodney Marsh and asked him why he thought that the NASL had failed to survive. He told me that the main problem had been over-investment. Basically the clubs had spent more than they could afford on players. Other factors that have been forwarded by observers include over-expansion, failure to secure a major television contract and over-reliance on foreign players. Whatever the reasons, after experiencing the excitement and vibrancy surrounding the Tampa Bay Rowdies soccer club in its halcyon days, I was really sad to hear of its demise.

But I digress. What about my summer of 1979? How did I go about salvaging something from the wreckage? I can't remember who approached whom, but I managed to make contact with one of the owners/directors of 'The Soccer Farm', a summer soccer camp based in Connecticut. Jim Kaufman (a university professor and soccer coach at Curry College, Milton, Massachusetts) ran the camp with his friend and partner in the venture Jim Kuhlmann (a school Phys. Ed. Instructor and soccer coach at Fairfield University, Connecticut).

Coming from an education background, and concerned to maintain the quality of their camp, they had a policy of only employing coaching staff who were both very good players and very good teachers. Apparently they had been struggling to find a US female to fit this description. Women's soccer in the US was definitely progressing at this time, with college women's varsity (inter-collegiate) programmes beginning to be established and funded by higher education institutions throughout the country. Curry College, where Jim Kaufman taught, was a case in point. In 1978, Jim had started the institution's first women's team as a recreational club. It became a varsity team (coached by Doug Williamson) in 1979. The first official AIAW (Association of Intercollegiate Athletics for Women) National Championship was still two years away, however, and according to Jim Kaufman: 'in 1979, there was still a great gap in terms of the availability of qualified and experienced female player/coaches in the USA.' When I told Jim about my background, I found myself bound for Connecticut and The Soccer Farm that coming July.

The residential camp was based at Pomfret School, a private boarding school near the small town of Pomfret, Connecticut. It was basically in the middle of nowhere, which was quite good for keeping the older children (and the counsellors and coaches for that matter) out of mischief! Not that anyone had the time or energy to get into trouble anyway, because the schedule, although very enjoyable, was a very demanding one. With the working day starting at about 9.30 a.m. and finishing around 10 p.m. and only one day off a week, between

12 noon on the Saturday, when one group of campers left and 1 p.m. on Sunday, when the next arrived, I was to live, eat and breathe soccer virtually 24/7 for the four weeks of my stay.

'Kuhls and Kauf', as the directors of the camp were affectionately known (this also helped to sort out any confusion as they were both called Jim), had started the camp in 1972, when it was called the Pomfret Soccer Clinic. Jim Kuhlmann, who in 1979 was in his early forties, had been an excellent player in his youth. While studying at Bridgeport University, he had captained the soccer team and played for the NCAA (National Collegiate Athletic Association) national first team. Both 'Kuhls' and 'Kauf' had coached college teams. They had also worked together at other soccer camps before starting their own. The camp's name had been changed to The Soccer Farm in the late 1970s and the slogan 'where the finest soccer players grow' adopted. This was indicative of the nurturing environment that they were trying to create, one in which young people came to camp and were encouraged to work hard to learn how to play better soccer, but at the same time to enjoy the process and have fun. Both aspects, learning and enjoyment, were considered to be of equal importance, especially as the children were paying customers and would not be coming back the next year if they hadn't had a good experience. Over the years, the Americans have become probably the best in the world at making soccer practice entertaining, and I was to gain many great ideas for fun, educational soccer games from my time at The Soccer Farm. This was something that the FA in England did not latch onto until considerably later.

The camp was extremely well organised. 'Kuhls and Kauf' had instituted a very efficient staff structure, which ensured that things ran smoothly. To oversee the coaching programme for the week they appointed one of the more experienced coaches to act as the programme co-ordinator. When I was at camp Ed Cannon, Dan Wilcox and Sandy Wilder rotated this role between them, each taking charge for a different week.

Ed Cannon was an excellent player. He had been an NCAA Division III All-American. He was also an accomplished coach and at the time was the soccer coach at St Anselm's College in New Hampshire. Dan Wilcox had been one of Jim Kuhlmann's players at Fairfield University. Since graduating, he had coached youth teams. Sandy Wilder played amateur soccer and was working as a coach at Principia College.

One of the roles of the programme co-ordinator was to hold daily team meetings involving all the coaches to evaluate what had gone on that day and plan for the next. Anyone could input into these meetings, it was all very informal and egalitarian. I found that I learnt a lot from discussing things with my colleagues and once again found my knowledge and viewpoint highly respected. I never got any sense of inferiority as the only woman coach; quite the opposite.

All the coaches that I worked with were excellent players and talented instructors. A few of those who spring to mind are Neville Lake, who was a talented soccer player and a private school soccer coach at Milton Academy; Gabriel Gomez, who had been a top player at Tufts University and was assistant coach to Jim Kaufman at Curry College; Tim Hunter and Ray Dezenzo. Ray was from Connecticut. He kindly invited me to stay with his family, for a short holiday after camp, before I flew home.

Another important person at camp was Jim Franco, who was the athletic trainer from Fairfield University. He provided important medical back-up by dealing with any injuries that were sustained by either staff or campers during the week.

Arguably the most important group in the staffing structure, however, were the camp counsellors, who were supervised by the head counsellor, Dan Woog. Dan was the assistant coach to Abie Loefler at Staples High School in Westport Connecticut. This was a very good school for soccer. Dan was also a talented writer and wrote for the soccer magazine, *Soccer America*. His job at camp involved giving the counsellors their assignments and schedule and evaluating their performance. He decided who had done a good job and should be invited back.

The counsellors' role was highly challenging. Theirs really was a twenty-four-hour job. At night, they had to supervise the children in the dormitories, sleeping in close proximity. By day they took charge of one particular group of children and followed them around all their activities, assisting the coaches on the field.

The counsellors were usually college students who were talented soccer players. Although I was the only female coach, there were some female counsellors, which was indicative of the fact that college women's soccer was getting started. It would only be a matter of time before these young women had gained enough experience to become good coaches themselves.

One of the first to do so was Lauren Gregg. She came from Jim Kaufman's home town of Wellesley, Massachusetts, where he had spotted her playing for a local team and invited her to come and work as a counsellor at The Soccer Farm. Laurie studied and played her soccer at the University of North Carolina, under the guidance of the future US Women's national team coach, Anson Dorrance. She was to enjoy considerable success as a player, as she played in the 1981 UNC team that won the first official AIAW National Championship, captained the side in the first NCAA Championship in 1982 and played for the US national team in 1986. In 1989 she became the first woman assistant coach to the US Women's national team and was with them through their highly successful World Cup and Olympic campaigns in the 1990s. In 1996, she was also made head coach of the US Under-20 Women's national team.

I am not sure how much The Soccer Farm could claim to have been an influence in her career, but she would certainly be included in any Hall of Fame of former campers and counsellors who have gone on to achieve great things. Others who might be included in this list were Paul Hunter, a camper who went on to play professional soccer for the New York Cosmos and Steve Bauman, who played for the Dallas Tornados. Like many others Bauman had literally grown up at The Soccer Farm, returning year after year as a camper and eventually becoming a counsellor.

Even more important to The Soccer Farm than its staff, were the campers. They were mainly upper-middle class children drawn primarily from the New England states. Many were from Fairfield County in Connecticut, where Jim Kuhlmann lived. According to Jim Kaufman, they had involved girls in their camp right from the outset, when they had represented less than twenty-five per cent of campers. The number had grown over the years, however, and judging from some of the team photographs that I still have, the ratio when I was coaching at The Soccer Farm was probably about two to one, male to female.

One of the things that I found particularly refreshing about coaching at The Soccer Farm (and in the USA in general) was that they had no qualms about teaching the boys and girls together in mixed groups. Back in England, I was still not able to persuade my school that the girls should be allowed to play football at all, let alone be pitched into competition with and against boys. At The Soccer Farm this seemed to work just fine. With the younger age groups it was never going to be a problem anyway. With the older children, an example of what they did to overcome any issues concerning physical differences was to bring the fifteen-to-sixteen-year-old girls to camp in the same week as the thirteen-to-fourteen-year-old boys. This solved a number of potential problems, both on and off the soccer field!

I was surprised to find that there were girls as young as seven at the camp, who were already really skilful little soccer players and as keen as mustard. They were really great to work with. Seemingly quite happy to be away from home for a week, they were really getting a great start in the game. They were being exposed to top-quality coaching and getting the opportunity to play soccer against girls and boys of their own age. There was nothing comparable for girls of this age in England at the time. Opportunities for girls to play in primary schools were rare. There were no summer camps and women's football clubs did not as yet have junior sections. It didn't take a genius to work out that the seeds being sown at the grass roots of girls' soccer development in the USA at the time were sooner or later almost bound to bear fruit.

The camp itself was set in beautiful surroundings. Pomfret School had lovely grounds, with a wide sweeping drive, leading through trees and past a smooth, grass soccer pitch, to the front door of the main building. This was several floors high and housed the dormitories and the staff accommodation. At the rear of the accommodation building there were more grass soccer pitches and an area of grass that had been marked out as mini soccer/tennis courts. These were left set up all the time and both children and staff used them at lunchtimes and in the evenings to play impromptu games. This was an enjoyable way to sharpen up your aerial control skills.

A building on the far side of these soccer fields housed the tuck shop. Jim Kuhlmann's teenage daughters Jodie, Kerri and Laurie came to camp to staff this. The kids could buy sweets, crisps and drinks from them at set times of the day.

Near the tuck shop building was the sports hall, which was very well used in the evenings. The children had an opportunity to play indoor soccer in there as part of the evening programme and, when they had finally been sent off to bed, the staff would take the opportunity to play. Staff games would usually get going at around 10.30 p.m., if we had any energy left. After making my presence felt in these games in the early part of the week I found that, as the week progressed, exhaustion set in and I had to opt for more gentle forms of relaxation!

The week's schedule was highly structured and well organised. It was also very demanding. I had never worked so hard in my life! Breakfast was at around 8 to 8.30 a.m. Everyone, campers and staff included, took meals in the nearby refectory. Once again I found institutional food to be more plentiful and varied than I had experienced back in England. Eggs, muffins, waffles with maple syrup and all manner of cereals and fruit were just some of the items on the menu for breakfast.

After breakfast the whole camp would assemble together at about 9.30 a.m. for a group warm-up. This was something that was also repeated after lunch, and was a good way of generating a bit of camp spirit, as well as preparing the children for the sessions that followed. The coaches would take it in turns to lead the warm up and there was always a bit of competition to see who could come up with the most enjoyable and novel activities. It was a great way to start the day.

The children would then break down into their teaching groups that they remained in for the whole week. Each group was assigned a counsellor, who would take them to their sessions and assist the coaches on the field.

There would be a couple of skills sessions in the morning, followed by a 'controlled scrimmage' (in England we would call it a conditioned game). This involved changing the rules slightly to emphasise a particular skill that the children had been working on in the morning session. This game would usually be coached.

After this there would be a fairly long break for lunch, during which there was usually a staff eleven-a-side match, on the pitch at the front of the school. The coaches all enjoyed playing in these games, but they were also considered educational for the children who were usually keen to watch. Hopefully it proved to them that their coaches could practise what they preached!

1 Early athletic prowess? About to take the plunge, Bognor, *c.* 1958.

2 The whole family, on the beach at Bognor, *c.* 1958. From left to right, back row: Uncle Fred, Mum, Dad holding one of my twin brothers, Grandad. Front row: my sister Viv, Mrs McCann with the other twin, Aunty Gertie, me.

3 Teenage sporting all-rounder. About to be presented with a doubles tennis trophy at the Beaconsfield Lawn Tennis Club summer tournament of 1971. I am at the front, on the right. My doubles partner, Julia Wassel, is on the far left.

4 Thame Ladies football team, 1971/72 season. From left to right, back row: Sally Walker, Nancy Roy, Jayne Hopkins, Bernadette Caswell, Tina Merrilees, Carol Mead. Front row: Shirley Entwistle, Alison East, me, Paddy McGroarty, Lynn Harris, Sandra French, Gillian Sayell. Maureen Dawson and Gloria Eele are missing from the photograph. (Courtesy of the *Bucks Advertiser*)

5 The 'Possibles' team, England national trial match, Leicester City's training ground, 17/9/72. I am on the back row, fifth from the left.

6 First official England team on the pitch at Wembley Stadium on 15/11/72, prior to travelling to Scotland for first international match on 18/11/72. From left to right, back row: Lynda Hale, Maggie Pearce (née Kirkland), Julia Brunton (née Manning), Paddy McGroarty, me, Sheila Parker (Captain), Jean Wilson, Sue Whyatt, Eric Worthington (Manager). Front row: Jeannie Allott, Janet Bagguley, Sue Buckett, Pat Davies, Eileen Foreman, Sylvia Gore, Sandra Graham.

7 The England team after beating France 3-0 away on 22/4/73. From left to right, back row: me, Lynda Hale, Sue Whyatt, Eileen Foreman, Sylvia Gore, Jeannie Allott, John Adams (Manager). Front row: Maggie Pearce (née Kirkland), Sheila Parker, Pat Davies, Sue Buckett, Janet Bagguley, Paddy McGroarty.

8 Playing a joke on the manager! Members of the England team pictured outside the team hotel prior to one of our home matches, c. 1973/74. From left to right, back row: Sue Lopez, Julia Brunton (née Manning), me, Maggie Miks, Sheila Parker. Front row: Tommy Tranter (Manager).

9 *Left:* Here I am taking a break during an England training session, *c.* 1973/74.

10 *Below:* The Netherlands tour in May 1974: let loose with my pals in Amsterdam! Left to right, standing: Sue Whyatt, Julia Brunton (née Manning), Jeannie Allott, me, Maggie Miks. Front: Janet Bagguley.

11 *Opposite above:* The stadium for our England game against Sweden in Gothenburg on 15/6/75.

12 *Opposite below:* Meeting up with some of the England men's football team for publicity during the Pony Home International Women's Football Championship in 1976. Left to right: Mick Channon, me, Gerry Francis.

13 *Left:* The England squad for the Pony Home International Championship, May 1976. From left to right, back row: Angela Poppy, -?-, Jane Talbot (physio), Rayner Hadden, Lorraine Dobb, -?-. Middle row: Flo Bilton (WFA official), Sue Buckett, Alison Leatherbarrow, Pat Firth, Pat Chapman, Carol McCune, Sue Lopez. Front row: Sylvia Gore (WFA official), Debbie Smith, Maggie Pearson (née Kirkland), Linda Coffin, Elaine Badrock, me.

14 *Left:* The England squad for the Pony Home International Championship, May 1976 with England manager Tommy Tranter (back row, far right), WFA official Flo Bilton (back row, far left) and press officer Roger Ebben (front row, far left).

15 *Below:* England manager Tommy Tranter gives the England team a dressing room team talk prior to a Pony Home International Championship match in May 1976. I am seated in the corner, seventh from the right.

16 Just about to embark on an England oversees tour, *c.* 1976. From left to right, back row: Elaine Badrock, me. Front row: Carol McCune, Linda Coffin, Pat Firth.

17 My cap for my first game for England against France on 22/4/73 and the commemorative trophy that I was presented with at the end of my career. All my caps are recorded on the small silver shields on the trophy. (Photographer: Steve Moore)

Members of the squad : Front row (left to right), Joannis Allot, Janet Beasley, Sue Buckett, Pat Davies, Eileen Foreman, Sylvia Gore and Sandra Graham. Back row (left to right), Lynda Hale, Moraz Kirkland, Julie Manning, Paddy McGroarty, Wendy Owen, Joan Wilson, Susan Whyatt, Shell: Parker (captain), and team manager Eric Worthington.

E·N·G·L·A·N·D!
The all girl squad
takes over Wembley

Story by GARTH BURDEN
Pictures by MONTY FRESCO

INTO the tackle . . . Paddy McGroarty shows how

! It's tough at the top

THOSE last few minutes in the Wembley dressing room are always the worst. It was the same yesterday. A quick dab of eyeshadow here, a smudged lipstick there, and 'Is my hair all right ?'

Then at last everyone was ready and it was down the tunnel to the roar of the crowds and on to the most famous football pitch in the world. England's first women's international football team was on the Wembley pitch. And loving every moment of it !

They were there for a training session in preparation for Saturday's first official women's international match.

Vital

And these schoolgirls, housewives, typists and students are determined to win. They intend to show a kind of Soccer format related to mere vital statistics.

The girls, aged between 15 and 28, shaped up well during training, and last night 10 of the team played a special five-a-side exhibition match during the National Five-a-Side Championships in London.

Saturday's big match against Scotland will be at Ravenscraig Park, Greenock. By Friday the team will be on its way from a training camp near Marlow, in Buckinghamshire, to the banks of the Clyde for an overnight stay at a hotel before the international.

Lone man

There is one man on the scene, however . . . the girls' trainer and team manager, FA staff coach Eric Worthington. His squad are :

GOALIES : Susan Buckett, 25, clerical supervisor of Gnibury Road, Aldesbury, Southampton ; Susan Whyatt, 16, schoolgirl, of Manchester.

FULL-BACKS : Sylvia Gore, 26, security officer, of Prescot, Lancashire ; Sandra Graham, 19, shorthand typist, of Blackpool ; Moraz Kirkland, 16, schoolgirl, from Kings-clare Avenue, Weston; Wendy Owen, 18, physical education student of Garvin Avenue, Boscombfield, and team captain Sheila Parker, 25, housewife, of Standish, nr. Wigan.

HALF-BACKS : Janet Baggaley, 17, typist, from Buxton, Derbyshire; Joan Wilson, 22, bank clerk, from Burnage, Manchester; Paddy Mc-Groarty, 24, booking clerk, from Stonehaven Road, Aylsbury.

STRIKERS : Joannis Allot, 16, schoolgirl, from Crewe; Pat Davies, 17, valuation clerk, from Priory Road, Netley Abbey, Hampshire; Eileen Foreman, 16, secretary, from Silver Street, Warminster, Wiltshire; Lynda Hale, 15, trainee machine operator, of Parchester Road, Woolston, Southampton; and Julia Manning, 21, of Oulton Broad, Lowestoft, Suffolk.

READY for the kick-off . . . and Wendy Owen gives the final touch to her eye make-up

18 The power of the press! That infamous, contrived *Daily Mail* photograph of me putting on eye make-up in the dressing room at Wembley Stadium prior to our training session on the hallowed turf on 15/11/72.

19 Rodney Marsh playing for the Tampa Bay Rowdies against Chicago Sting in 1978.

20 Staff at The Soccer Farm in Pomfret, Connecticut, USA, c. 1979. Left to right: Jim Kuhlmann, Ed Cannon, Jim Franco.

21 Female counsellors at The Soccer Farm, Connecticut, c. 1979. Left to right: Polly Kaplan, Margo Petukian, Alicia Camillo.

22 A children's team that I was coach to for the week at The Soccer Farm, c. 1979.

23 Tampa Stadium, home to the Tampa Bay Rowdies, when I coached for them in the summer of 1978.

24 The Dartford College women's football team that reached the quarter-finals of the WFA Cup in the 1976/77 season. From left to right, back row: Laura Greenfield, Sandie O'Toole, Janet Bickerstaffe (aka Charlie Brown), me, Belinda ?, Lorraine Everard, Ann Whatley (trainer). Front row: Sue Peck, Jill Powell, Shirley Reynolds, Chris Davies, Sandy Tolen.

25 My other sport. Giving the Carnegie netball team some coaching tips at half-time during the British Colleges netball final at Lilleshall National Sports Centre in 1982.

Wendy's wealth of experience so valuable

GIRLS ON FILM: Tranmere U16s girls' football team before their recent match against Brighton & Hove Albion at Stanney High School.
9826SB2A

26 The 2000/01 Under-16 squad at the FA Centre of Excellence for Girls at Tranmere Rovers. Back row, far left is Sylvia Gore (Centre Co-ordinator), far right is me (Squad Coach). (Picture courtesy of *Ellesmere Port Pioneer*)

27 With Michael Owen at the AXA coaching day at Chester City FC in 2001.

28 *Left:* With Emile Heskey at the AXA coaching day at Chester City FC in 2001.

29 *Below:* A thank you for my coaching, from the highly successful Chester College women's football team of 2001/02. (Courtesy of universityphotographer.co.uk)

30 Members of the 2002/03 Under-14 squad from the Sport Cheshire Advanced Coaching Centre at University College Chester. (Courtesy of Jeff Price, Chronicle Newspapers)

31 The 2003/04 Under-12 squad from the Sport Cheshire Advanced Coaching Centre for Girls' Football, based at University College Chester. The picture was taken at the end-of-season tournament in Bolton, with centre coaches Sarah Burnyeat (back row, far left), Kym Gaskell (back row, second from the right) and myself (back row, far right).

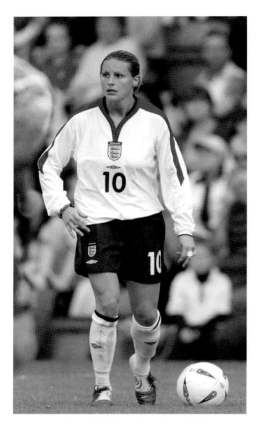

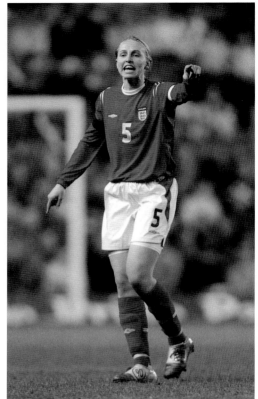

Clockwise from top left:

32 Kelly Smith, one of England's top strikers, pictured in action in 2004.

33 Faye White, current England captain, pictured in action against Iceland in May 2004.

34 The England squad at the La Manga training camp, January 2005.

I felt that it was particularly important for me to participate on these occasions, to give the girls at the camp an example to follow. In researching this book, I asked Jim Kaufman what sort of impression I had made with my performances on the field of play. He said: 'you had the skills of a very, very good soccer player. You had game sense and a presence on the field. We could tell that we were watching someone play, who knew what they were doing.' He added: 'you were the kind of role model that girls need to have, so that they can learn that they can do what the boys do.'

Apparently, one of the things that I could do in the same way as the boys was to skilfully take the ball out of the air and chest trap it to the ground. According to Jim Kaufman, when they first saw me do this, they were all amazed as they had never seen a woman chest trap a ball properly before. Jim recalls that, at the time, there was concern in the USA about girls getting hit in the chest. It was therefore common practice for the rules for girls' soccer competitions to allow girls to put their hands across the chest as protection, and to trap the ball on the forearms. They obviously didn't continue to allow this in subsequent years and I like to think that maybe I helped to start the revolution!

After the staff match was over, and the coaches had enjoyed a little recovery time, the afternoon programme began. This followed a similar format to the morning, with the coaches assigned to a different skills station to avoid boredom. The children moved around the stations under the guidance of their counsellor. Once again the afternoon finished with a controlled scrimmage and then it was time for a meal and some relaxation before the evening programme commenced.

This was the part of the day that the children really looked forward to, because it was when they got the opportunity to play 'a proper game' in a competitive evening league. Teams were picked at the beginning of the week and assigned a coach who would work with them for the duration. There were two matches every evening, which were refereed by the counsellors. Coaches would pick their team, give a talk beforehand and then encourage from the sidelines. The kids loved it because they were playing in a 'real match' and enjoyed getting to know their coach. We coaches found it fun too. There was always a bit of good-natured rivalry between us. You were secretly quite proud if your team ended the week as the champions!

After the evening programme was over the children were handed over to the counsellors, who had the unenviable job of settling them down and getting them off to bed. The idea was that, because we had worked them hard through a long, hot day, they would be exhausted and fall asleep very easily. Unfortunately this rarely seemed to work and more often than not it was the counsellors and the coaches who were on their knees through tiredness! Our day wasn't over yet. There was still the staff meeting to attend. This usually took place at about 9.30 p.m. After this, however, the high point of the day finally arrived: PIZZA!

We were all really hungry by now, because we had eaten our evening meal at about 5.30 p.m. So every night we would send out for takeaway pizza. We phoned our order through and then sent a volunteer to pick it up and bring it back to the common room. The giant boxes of pizza would then be opened up and spread around the floor for everyone to share. We also passed around cold drinks, which were kept in a big icebox in the kitchen. I thought that this was fantastic because American pizza wasn't widely available in England at the time. I had never seen such huge pizzas, with such a wide variety of toppings. Pizza time was our relaxing part of the day, when the staff could eat, chat and have a laugh together, without the company of children. It was bliss.

After that, some coaches would play indoor soccer; others would go and relax in their rooms. On the odd occasion we might forego the pizza and smarten ourselves up for a trip into Pomfret for an evening at a bar/restaurant. This was a rare treat, however, as we were usually too tired to make the effort.

The week ended on a Saturday, when the parents came to collect their children at around 12 noon. We then had time off until the next group arrived at 1 p.m. the next day. This wasn't much time to do anything in, but if you had planned to go off camp for the weekend, you could sometimes get away a little earlier. I did manage several outings during my time at The Soccer Farm. The first was to Boston, which was a city that I had always wanted to visit. I teamed up with a couple of the other coaches for the day to explore the tourist sights. In the evening we went to see the New England Teamen (as Boston's NASL soccer team was called) play in a floodlit league game. We obviously couldn't last a whole day without any soccer!

During our day in Boston we decided to follow 'The Freedom Trail'. You follow a painted line all around the streets of the city, as it takes you to all the venues associated with the city's role in the struggle for independence from the English. Whoever had this idea was a genius. We spent a very enjoyable day wandering around without once having to ask for directions. They should try this out in some of England's historic cities. The soccer game in the evening was fun, but it didn't match up to the excitement, or scale, of a visit to Tampa Stadium to see the Rowdies play. I had been spoilt by that experience.

One of my other weekend jaunts was to Rhode Island, which is a state east of Connecticut. I was invited to go there with one of the American coaches for an overnight stay, with him and his partner, at their weekend retreat. They were very keen to entertain a visitor from England. As we drove there, I was looking forward to a relaxing experience to set me up for the next week at camp. Rhode Island is famous for its fish, and their speciality is clams. These are caught and sold fresh, from various stalls down by the shore. Although I had never eaten clams before, as my hosts were so keen to cook me a nice fish meal that evening, I resolved to give them a try. I have to say that the meal itself was delicious, but not very long after we had eaten my nightmare began.

I suddenly began to feel very nauseous and disappeared to the bathroom, where I began to be violently sick. I thought that once I had thrown up I would be okay, but it was not to be. The vomiting went on and on and on, until I was in a very bad way. Eventually my worried hosts came to find me and obviously didn't like what they saw. They immediately phoned the hospital and were told to get me down to the emergency department as soon as possible. A flashing light was produced from somewhere and stuck on the roof of the truck and I was soon being rushed downtown. Once the doctors got hold of me they quickly diagnosed clam poisoning, a severe, adverse reaction to that type of shellfish and gave me an injection to stop the vomiting. They put me on a drip to get some fluids into me and then, later on, when I was more recovered, they sent me home.

The funny side of this story (although I couldn't see it at the time) was that they gave my hosts some suppositories and a rubber glove to take away with them, with instructions concerning what they were to do with them! These were people that I hardly knew and needless to say I decided to administer my own medication!

I was sufficiently recovered by the next day to travel back to camp, but would need a day off before I started work again. It had hardly been the relaxing break that I had been hoping for. When we got back to The Soccer Farm we had a good laugh recounting the tale and showing off the medical equipment that we had brought back with us!

The programme at the camp followed the same format each week, but was never boring as the age range of the children varied. The oldest children attended in the final week, for instance. As this approached its conclusion, I had mixed feelings about my impending departure. I was looking forward to a well-earned rest as I was by now thoroughly exhausted after such a demanding schedule. On the other hand, once I had been home for a while and recovered, I knew that I would miss the people and the place.

Although I had initially been disappointed that I was not going back to work for the Tampa Bay Rowdies that summer, by the end of it, I had no regrets whatsoever. Working at The Soccer Farm had been a great experience and had more than compensated for anything else that I might have missed. I had learnt so much from 'Kuhls and Kauf' and the other coaches about how to organise a coaching programme for children that was educational and fun. I was taking away some innovative ideas that I would be able to use in my coaching and teaching back home. It had also been interesting to witness how girls' and women's soccer was progressing, with more young girls than ever attending camp and the older ones coming through as counsellors. As I flew back home to England, I was already looking forward to the next year.

I was to enjoy another stint at The Soccer Farm in the summer of 1980, unaware that this was in fact to be my last coaching assignment in the USA. After that, I had less time to spare in the summer holidays, because I was attempting to make a career move from school teaching to college lecturing and had further qualifications to pursue.

In the academic year 1981/82, I had spent an enjoyable year lecturing on a temporary contract at Leeds Polytechnic's Carnegie School of Physical Education and Sport. This was, at the time, one of the top college sports departments in the country. I knew, however, that if I wanted to find a permanent job in the higher education sector, I would need to obtain a Master's degree.

I did initially apply to do this in the USA, as I saw this as a perfect opportunity to combine soccer coaching with my studies. The only way that I was going to be able to afford this, however, was to find a university that would accept me as a student and give me an assistant soccer coach's job to fund my stay. I very nearly pulled it off. I received a phone call, at Carnegie, from a college in New York State that wanted me as the assistant coach for their varsity women's soccer team. I would also be able to register for their Sports Science Master's degree. They were pretty confident that they could get around US employment law by writing a job description that would only fit me. Everything was looking rosy until I had a last-minute phone call to tell me that unfortunately they had interviewed a suitable US candidate for the post and could not therefore (even though they wanted to) give the job to me. That was effectively the end of my American dream. I ended up doing a Master of Arts degree in England instead and embarked upon a college lecturing career in this country.

I lost my connection with the USA until the late 1990s, when I established a work-experience link for my college students with a soccer education company called UK Elite, which is based in New Jersey. This led to me making my first trip back to the States in eighteen years.

In my absence, women's soccer in the USA had rocketed. Since 1980, when I had last coached at The Soccer Farm, there had been a huge growth in female participation at youth and amateur levels and college women's soccer had really taken off. Soccer scholarships had become available for women on an equal basis to men and were very sought after as a way of funding a player's higher education. Girls had begun to train hard in schools in order to earn them. As good players began to come through the education system, the first US Women's national team had been formed in 1985, losing in that same year to our far more experienced England women's side. By 1991, however, the USA Women's soccer team had won the first women's World Cup, following this up in 1996 with an Olympic gold. The team's star player of the 1990s, Mia Hamm, had been named one of the world's most beautiful people, had seen a Nike building named after her and was making more than £1.5 million a year through product endorsements. As one of the very first females to have been employed to coach soccer in the USA, I couldn't help feeling that I had been really unlucky to have missed the party!

six

Coaching Football in England 1973-1992

The climate that I faced as a female football coach in England in the 1970s and early 1980s was very different to the one that I had experienced on my visits to the USA. Trying to convince the education establishment in this country that football was a suitable game for girls and young women and one that should be included in the programme was a bit of an uphill battle. I did experience some success in introducing a women's football team at my teacher training college at Dartford. I had less impact, however, in my first teaching job at a mixed comprehensive school in the Medway Towns. To appreciate what I was up against, it might help to know a little bit about the traditions within girls and women's physical education at that time.

DARTFORD COLLEGE WOMEN'S FOOTBALL TEAM, 1973-1977

In 1972, when I began my Certificate in Education course at Dartford College, it was one of the top specialist women's physical education colleges in England. Its main rivals were Bedford, Chelsea, which was actually in Eastbourne, and I.M. Marsh in Liverpool. These were single-sex establishments. Dartford had recently gone co-ed on some other courses, but the PE course was still strictly for women only. It had a long history of training young women to go out into the nation's secondary schools to provide young girls with a sound and healthy physical education.

Dartford was unique, as it was the very first of these colleges to be established in this country. Founded in 1885 by a Swedish educationalist called Madame Osterberg, the curriculum in the early days was heavily influenced by the teachings of another Swede, P.H. Ling, who believed in the value of therapeutic gymnastics for improving posture and health. As well as gymnastics, the curriculum followed by 'Madame's girls' (which is what the young ladies who attended the college were known as by the local people) would have included anatomy and physiology, dance, swimming, music, drama and some suitable games.[1] The latter included lacrosse, hockey and a game which was apparently invented by the students at Madame Osterberg's – net ball (*sic*).

Net ball was adapted from a game called basketball, which was demonstrated to Madame's girls by an American (Dr Toles), who visited the college in 1895. The students subsequently modified its rules by dividing the court into three sections and introducing rings and nets instead of baskets. A more genteel version of the original basketball game, netball (as it was later spelt) went on to become hugely popular as a national sport for girls and women.

Even the playing of these types of games by young women caused consternation in the late 1800s and early 1900s, however. In 1892, Madame Osterberg had introduced the knee-length gym tunic, to allow her girls greater freedom of movement. This was a big improvement on the restrictive corsets that women had up until then been obliged to wear while exercising in order to satisfy standards of decorum and decency. The sight of Madame's girls running around playing games in this relatively skimpy attire caused great uproar, however, and articles and photographs highlighting this disgraceful practice appeared in the national press!

Things had obviously moved on a bit from this by the time that I arrived at Dartford College (formerly known as The Bergman Osterberg Physical Training College) in the early 1970s, but in some respects very little had changed. Many of the older people in the local community still, in fact, referred to us as Madame's girls, even though our founder had been dead for over fifty years! Some members of the teaching staff were still very posture conscious. I can remember mine being criticised during my interview for a place at Dartford. I came away really worried that I would be rejected because of my shortcomings in this area.

The college curriculum had broadened slightly to include aspects such as athletics and a wider range of games but, apart from this, was very similar to that described above. Netball, lacrosse and hockey were still the mainstays of the winter games programme. Of these, netball was the sport for which Dartford was most renowned. This was the game that the students had invented and they didn't like to be beaten at it. Dartford prided itself on winning the British Colleges Netball Championships every year. This was my other main sport, which I pursued very seriously alongside my football. By the end of my three years at college, I was very proud to have won a British Colleges medal with the college first netball team and to have been selected to play for Kent Seniors and the Welsh Under-21s.

There was no place for football on the curriculum at Dartford, or any of the other women's PE colleges at that time, however. This was understandable as, in England, the game was still regarded as a traditionally male, working-class sport and was not included on the curriculum for girls in schools. It was unsurprising, therefore, that it was not to be found as part of the programme at a predominantly female, middle-class teacher training establishment.

It was against this backdrop that I set out to break years of tradition, by starting the first ever women's football team at Dartford College. It was probably also one of the first, if not the first, college women's teams to be formed in the whole of England.

Our first season was in 1973/74, when I was in my second year at college. In my first year I had tried to go home at weekends to continue playing for Thame Ladies, who were by then in the First Division of the Home Counties League. It was important for me to be playing regular competitive football, to keep my game up to standard for continued selection for the England team but, with my other sporting and college commitments, Thame was proving much too far to travel to regularly. The obvious answer was to form a student club at college.

I was aided in this venture by my England status that, although initially regarded with some scepticism by the principal, had subsequently received positive support from the college governors. Another very important factor was the appointment of a new male head of PE, to join the otherwise predominantly female physical education department. John Johnstone was a keen footballer and was very supportive of the team's endeavours. He also offered very tangible help, by agreeing to referee our home games. We had to play these off campus, as the college playing fields were not marked out for football. We either travelled to the Thames Polytechnic Sports Ground, (when Dartford became part of the polytechnic) or, for important cup games, sometimes managed to gain access to Dartford Football Club, which was quite a good little ground.

To get the team up and running, I initially cajoled some of my friends and the girls that I knew were good hockey players into coming along to practice to have a go at the sport. The hockey players had no trouble grasping the tactical side of the game because of its obvious similarities to their sport. As there were no other colleges that I knew of that were playing women's football, I entered the team into the Kent women's league and the WFA Cup. Games were played on a Sunday, so they didn't clash with the netball, hockey and lacrosse fixtures, which were played on a Saturday.

Our games in the Kent League were often bruising encounters, played against predominantly working-class, local teams, whose players thought that it was great sport to come and try to knock the stuffing out of Madame's girls. Madame's girls we may have been, but we were no pushover. We had some very talented players and more than held our own in the league. The only problem that we had was trying to fulfil all our fixtures. The league didn't stop for college holidays and we often fell behind and ended up giving other teams the points. This didn't make us very popular with the league's organisers but I did manage to placate them by offering my playing and coaching services to the league representative team.

In the WFA Cup, we were one of eighty-nine clubs from all over the country who had entered the competition in the 1973/74 season.[2] These were organised into eight regional groups with the top two teams from each group proceeding to the last sixteen. Our group included a total of eleven teams from the Kent and Sussex area. As we were a new club, playing in our first competitive season, we predictably didn't get beyond the group stages that year. It was all good experience though and we needed to be playing in this top competition if we were going to improve. The following season (1974/75) we did slightly better, but lost 9-1 in the final stages of the group. After that result, I knew that we needed to be better organised in future, if we were to have any chance against the big guns of women's football. I can remember doing a lot of coaching work on set plays. I went over and over everyone's positions on corners and free-kicks. I not only did this on the training ground but also drew diagrams on paper and circulated them around the team bus on the way to games, just to make sure.

Something must have paid off, because in the 1976/77 season (I had left college by then but was still eligible to play) Dartford College had a fantastic WFA Cup run to reach the quarter-finals of the competition. Reaching the last eight in a season when entries had increased to reach 107[3] was a great achievement in itself. Our opponents were to be the mighty Southampton Ladies. The best team in women's football at that time, they were holders of the WFA Cup and had appeared in every final of the six that had taken place since the competition's inception in 1971, winning on five of those occasions.

There were advantages to having been drawn against Southampton. Firstly it would be great to have a crack at beating the best team in the country and as the real underdogs we would have absolutely nothing to lose. It was a bit like Accrington Stanley drawing Manchester United in the FA Cup. Secondly, of all the teams that we could have played, Southampton Ladies was the one that I knew most about, as five of their team had been my colleagues in the England team for the previous five years. I had also played against Southampton on various occasions in the past, as a member of Thame Ladies Football Club. Thame had lost to them in the WFA Cup semi-final in 1972, but drawn with them to share the Home Counties League Cup in 1973.

All in all, I was extremely excited to be playing against the old enemy again. The forthcoming clash also sparked interest in the local press, with an article, including pictures of the team, appearing in the *Kentish Times*, in the run-up to the game.

I can remember our strategy for the game and how events unfolded on the day in more detail than I can remember any game of football that I ever played in. This was probably because, on this occasion, I was the player/manager, responsible for making all the decisions on how we might overcome the enormous odds and try to achieve a famous victory.

Southampton had great players all over the field, but two of the greatest threats were their wingers. They had Lynda Hale on the right and Pat Chapman on the left, both of whom were England internationals. They needed to be contained so that they couldn't supply crosses into the middle, where they had threat number three, England centre forward Pat Davies! As an England central defender, I hoped that I would be able to cope with Pat Davies, but I needed to find a way to keep the wingers quiet. I decided that our left-back Sue Peck (better known as Speck) wouldn't have a chance against Lynda Hale if she allowed Lynda to receive the ball with space to turn and run with it. I knew that Lynda was deadly in this situation, as I had seen her 'skin' the fullback many a time when she was playing with me for England. My instructions to Speck were: 'stay right up that winger's backside all the time and whatever you do don't let her turn with the ball to face you!' I really drummed this into her. In an attempt to deal with Pat Chapman on the left, I decided, before the game, to make a positional switch and swap our right-back (Pip Newnham) and our right midfielder (Sandra Tolen) around. Pip was faster in the sprint than Sandy and I thought it would be a good idea for her to engage their left winger earlier, higher up the pitch, to keep her away from the danger area. I reasoned that with her speed she would be able to recover quickly behind Sandy if she was beaten.

Southampton had another England player, in midfield, in the shape of Sue Lopez. She was very good at coming forward to join the attack, so she needed to be watched. We had two excellent midfielders of our own, in Lorraine Everard and Laura Greenfield, however, who I hoped would be able to cancel her out. As well as all their attacking riches, Southampton also had a very strong defence, which included the England left-back Maggie Kirkland and the England goalkeeper Sue Buckett. We were going to have to make the most of the few opportunities that we would get to score. Our centre forward Sandie O'Toole was a quality striker however, who was one of the few players in the team to have played for a football team before coming to college (her other claim to fame was that she was a Great Britain javelin thrower). We also had Gill Powell up front, who, as one of the very talented Powell twins, could turn her hand to any sport.

Another thing that we had going for us, was the home advantage. On the day (20 February 1977) a good crowd of student supporters were transported to the Thames Polytechnic sports ground from Dartford College to cheer us on. My

Mum and Dad also travelled down from Buckinghamshire, which was great because I always valued my Dad's opinion at half-time. He was a great reader of the game and it was sometimes a little difficult for me to see everything as well as concentrating on playing my own game.

We were a little nervous before the game kicked off but as a team we were determined not to be overawed by the reputation of the Southampton Ladies. We had a plan and were determined to try to make it work. As the first half progressed it became apparent that Speck was doing a fantastic job on Lynda Hale. She stuck to her like glue and every time Lynda received the ball, Speck was right up behind her, as instructed, snapping at her heels like a terrier. Southampton were getting no joy on that flank at all. Their left-hand side was a different story, however. My decision to switch our right-back and right midfield player around was not paying off. Both Sandy and Pip were uncomfortable playing out of position and Pat Chapman was able to capitalise on this. By about twenty-five minutes or so into the game, Southampton had scored two goals, both from moves instigated by Pat Chapman down their left wing. In an attempt at damage limitation, I quickly switched our two right-sided players back into their usual positions. This seemed to do the trick. Before very long we had the Southampton attack far more contained and were able to start making some moves of our own.

Slowly but surely we started to claw our way back into the game. We got one goal back to narrow the margin and then, against all the odds, we scored a second to draw level at two goals each. This was beyond my wildest dreams. With not very long to go in the match the minnows from Dartford College were matching the Southampton Ladies (England internationals and all)! At that point we really didn't look like losing and even had a few chances to finish the game off ourselves. Just when I thought that we were going to hold on until the final whistle, disaster struck. Southampton mounted a last-ditch attack and the ball broke to Sue Lopez, who was supporting the forwards from midfield. She was within shooting range but still quite a long way from the goal. I moved to close her down, so that she couldn't get any closer. As I did so, she elected to shoot. Her shot was a fairly innocuous one really. As the ball went past me, I turned to watch its flight. I remember thinking: 'Oh, that's okay, Shirley will deal with that.' I can only think that our goalkeeper, Shirley Reynolds, was unsighted, or the ball bobbled at the last minute, because somehow it managed to evade her grasp and end up in the back of the net. It was a devastating blow for all of us (not least our poor 'keeper) but there was no time to dwell on it then. We quickly picked the ball out of the net and ran it back to the centre spot. There wasn't much time left and we were desperate to try to level it again.

Unfortunately it was not to be. We had made a gallant and inspired attempt, but when the final whistle went, we had been beaten by the narrowest of margins at three goals to two. We were all hugely disappointed but, really, giving Southampton such a close game was a fantastic achievement. There were not many teams in England who ever managed to give Southampton (in their pomp) a run for their money. After beating us in the quarter-final they progressed to their seventh WFA Cup final, where they lost 1-0 to QPR.

After I had got over the deflation at having been so near yet so far and had taken time to reflect on our performance, I was very proud of what we had all achieved that day. Everyone had played their hearts out. No individual was to blame for our defeat, least of all our goalkeeper, who had made some excellent saves throughout the match, to keep us in contention. If anything, it was my tactical decision to switch things around on our right flank that had been a contributing factor in our downfall, as this had effectively given Southampton a two-goal head start. We had done really well to come back from this and, when I think of that quarter-final WFA Cup match now, it stands out in my memory not as a disappointing experience but as the Dartford College Women's football team's finest hour (and a half)!

I like to think that in setting up and running the team at the college in the 1970s, I made some contribution towards the development of women's football in the education sector at that time. Hopefully, I challenged some of the more traditional views concerning the suitability of the sport for women. At the very least, the fact that football was made available to the female students at the college, as another extra-curricular club, gave them a chance to enjoy and learn the skills of the sport. Some of Dartford's players did then pass this enjoyment on to others by starting girls' teams in the schools that they went out to teach in after leaving college.

I also like to think that Madame Osterberg herself would have been proud of these achievements. After all, she was not just a physical educator. She was a pioneer, who championed the cause of female emancipation and sent her girls out 'to change the world for women.'

THE HUNDRED OF HOO BOYS' FOOTBALL TEAM, 1975-1978

I went out from Dartford College in June 1975. Armed with my prestigious certificate (Dartford was renowned as a top-class teacher training institution) I applied for and was offered a post as an assistant teacher of physical education at the Hundred of Hoo School, on the Isle of Grain in Kent. This was close to the towns of Rochester, Chatham and Gillingham, which are collectively known as the Medway Towns, after the river Medway, on which they are all situated.

I initially secured lodgings in Rochester, which was only about thirty or forty minutes away from Dartford. This enabled me to continue as player/coach to the college women's team for several years after I had started teaching. As well as working with adults, I was also keen to get involved in coaching children and enquired about the possibility of starting a girls' football team at my school. I can't remember exactly who put the block on this idea, but I know that I was actively discouraged from doing this, because it was not considered to be a suitable game for the girls to be involved in. I was told that there would be no objection to me coaching one of the boys' teams, however.

With the benefit of hindsight, I should probably have pushed a little harder to get a girls' team approved, or at the very least abstained, on principle, from coaching the boys, when the girls weren't allowed to take part. In my defence, however, I was a young teacher embarking on a demanding probationary year. I probably didn't have the confidence at that stage in my career to rock the boat. Consequently, I did decide to take on the role of coach to the under-thirteen boys' football team at the Hundred of Hoo School. This was to be my first experience of working with a boys' team. It proved to be a highly positive one, which broadened my horizons. From this starting point, I went on to enjoy coaching both male and female footballers, at various camps and educational establishments that I was employed at, over many years.

Fortunately I didn't experience any problems in gaining the respect of my boys' team at the Hundred of Hoo School. They all knew that I was a qualified coach and played football for England, which probably helped. They seemed very keen to work with me to become better players and a successful team.

The only time that I ever heard any derogatory comments about me being a woman and coaching a boys' team was from our opponents at other schools. On one particular occasion, we were playing away in nearby Chatham and some of the boys in the other team started teasing my lads about having a woman in charge, to try to psyche them out before the game. I overheard a couple of my boys retaliate by saying: 'Well our coach plays for England and she's better than yours any day.' My team then went on to do their talking on the pitch. If my memory serves me correctly, we went on to win that game by at least a two or three-goal margin!

Another thing that gave me some kudos with the boys was the fact that they had seen me hold my own, as the only female member of the staff football team. This team was drawn from all different departments in the school – even the deputy head played. We used to have an annual challenge match against the senior pupils, which the whole school came out to watch. This was in the days before this type of activity was stopped for fear of pupil injury and possible litigation. Everyone really enjoyed this event, which was highly entertaining and good for staff-student relations.

In addition to the staff/pupil match, the team played regular fixtures against other staff teams from schools in the local area. No one seemed to be the slightest bit fazed by the fact that there was a woman playing for the Hundred of Hoo team. The FA did not approve of mixed football, because of the physical differences between males and females and the threat of injury. This never proved to be a problem in our matches, however, as I always made myself aware of any opponent with a physical frailty and went easy on him in the tackle! I was in fact often one of the strongest players (both physically and in terms of ability) on the pitch in these fixtures, as quite a few of the teachers who played staff football were fairly slight men, who were keen to play but not necessarily very sporty.

I remained as coach to the Hundred of Hoo boys' football team for several years, as they progressed from under-thirteen through to the under-fifteen age group. I eventually handed them over to another teacher when I felt that they were getting older and probably in need of a fresh face. The time that I had spent working with them was very enjoyable. There were some very talented players in the squad, who were always highly motivated and worked hard for me at practice. The team achieved some good results and was usually highly placed in the league. Over the years the other schools that we played against became used to seeing me and ceased to tease my boys about having a woman coach. They knew that as opponents, we would always be well organised and very tough to beat.

During the five years that I taught physical education at the Hundred of Hoo School (from 1975 to 1980) I played for England, coached a boys' school team and was invited to the USA to coach for the Tampa Bay Rowdies. I may not have succeeded in introducing girls' football at the school, but hopefully I did at least raise awareness of the fact that a woman could be a very good player and a successful coach.

FA PRELIMINARY CERTIFICATE FOR COACHING: COLDHARBOUR SPORTS CENTRE, ELTHAM, 1980

As a result of all the experience that I had gained as a coach during the 1970s (both in England and the USA), as the 1980s began, I decided that the time was right for me to further my football coaching qualifications. I had held the WFA Preliminary Coaching Certificate since 1974 and was keen to try to gain the FA Full Qualifying Award (the so-called 'Full Badge'), which was the equivalent of today's 'A' Licence.

In order to be eligible to apply for this I had to jump through a few hoops first. Initially I would have to take the FA Preliminary Certificate Course, a virtually identical course to the WFA version. I would then need to enrol on a

Preparatory Course and be recommended from that to apply for the Full Badge Course. The FA didn't believe in making things easy! All this was obviously going to require a big commitment in terms of both time and energy.

In May 1980, I enrolled on a Prelim Course that was to take place at Coldharbour Sports Centre in Eltham. The main difference between this course and the one that I had taken at Lilleshall in 1974 was that whereas the latter had been women only, in Eltham I was to be the only woman on the course! This was to become the norm on most of the FA courses that I subsequently attended.

The course proved to be a big challenge for me. Although I had already passed the WFA version, this had been undertaken in an environment where I was surrounded by my peers from women's football and taught by the England women's team manager Tommy Tranter, who knew what I was capable of as a player. I now had to prove myself as the only woman on an FA course, where I didn't know any of the other candidates or the tutor. This was also taking place at a time when the FA had not yet fully embraced the women's game. The WFA had been recognised by the FA in 1972, but would not become fully affiliated to it until 1983. The FA would not go on to take over the running of women's football until 1993.

I knew that the pass rate on FA Preliminary Coaching Certificate courses was not particularly high and I felt that I was going to need to be twice as good as the men to have a chance of gaining the award. This was my perception going into the course. I definitely felt conspicuous and different to start with, but as the course progressed and I got to know the other players and the tutor, I began to feel accepted as 'one of the lads'. I was a better player than some of the men in the group, which gained me the respect and support of my colleagues.

There was, in general, a great sense of camaraderie among the candidates, which is something that I have always found to be the case on FA coaching award courses. A tacit reciprocal agreement usually exists, whereby you work hard in other people's sessions so that they will return the favour in yours. Everyone is in the same boat and appreciates the pressure that the person doing their assessed coaching session is under.

The lads certainly worked hard for me in my practice sessions. For the final assessment, however, a group of young boys was brought in for us to coach. I was really nervous and not convinced that I would be able to motivate them to work for me. In the event, everything seemed to go smoothly. I am sure that I benefited from the fact that I had already had three years' experience in coaching a boys' football team.

You are never quite sure how you have done on these occasions, however, until you get the results. In this case, they were sent in the post. When I opened the letter I was delighted to find that I had been awarded the certificate, with a pass in 'Practical Coaching' and 'Practical Performance' and a good pass in 'Theory of Coaching' and 'Laws of the Game'.

FA PREPARATORY COACHING COURSE: BISHAM ABBEY NATIONAL SPORTS CENTRE, APRIL 1981

With my FA Prelim under my belt, the following year I embarked on the next step towards the Full Badge by attending a three-day Preparatory Course at Bisham Abbey. This was a venue that I was quite familiar with as I had stayed there in 1972 with the England women's football team in the build up to our first ever international match. This time, however, I did not live in, as my parents' home was nearby. Quite a few male professional and ex-professional players, who were trying to make the transition into coaching, attended the course. Once again, I was the lone female.

The course tutors were Robin Russell, who has since risen to the dizzy heights of technical co-ordinator at the FA and Colin Murphy, who was the FA regional coach for London (North). The content was a big step up from the Prelim and prepared us for the type of work that we could expect to be involved in on a Full Qualifying Award course. It involved a lot of coaching in eight versus eight small-sided game situations and phases of play.

In order to be recommended for the Full Badge course, I felt that it was going to be important not only to get to grips with the material and impress in my practical coaching sessions, but also to give a good account of myself as a player. The latter is not easy when you are the only woman playing against quality male players. I can remember that the timing of the course was towards the end of a season when I had been training particularly hard with my club (Maidstone Ladies) and was super-fit. This definitely helped me to cope with sessions where I played with and against male professionals, whom I found to be very supportive.

Looking back, a very interesting and telling point emerges from the outcome of this course. At the end of the three days, the tutors (Robin and Colin) told me that they felt that I was ready to undertake a Full Badge course. They did, however, inform me that before I applied, it would be necessary for them to consult Allen Wade, the then-director of coaching at the FA, to see if he would consent to me, as a woman, enrolling on the course. This surprised me at the time and I was worried that after all my hard work I would not be able to progress. The fact that the tutors felt the need to seek permission for me to do so was indicative of the fact that a woman had yet to take part in a Full Qualifying Award Course. As a consequence, the FA had not had to address the place of women in the higher echelons of the coaching structure. I went away to await a decision, which arrived in a letter from Colin Murphy, dated 10 April 1981. It read as follows:

Dear Wendy,

Further to our conversation at Bisham Abbey after the Preparatory Course held last week, I have discussed your desire to attend a Full Qualifying Award Course with Mr Allen Wade, Director of Coaching at the Football Association. He sees no reason why you should not undertake the course, providing you fully understand the commitment you are making both from a coaching and playing point of view. Therefore, you should go ahead with an application as intended.

I had received the green light to attend the FA's most prestigious coaching award course. This may not seem like much now, but, for a female who had experienced being banned from playing on FA-affiliated pitches in the 1960s, at the time it felt like a ground-breaking achievement.

One of my biggest regrets in life will always be that I didn't actually go on to attend the course until almost twenty years later. I should have taken it straight away, while I was young, still playing competitive football and at my peak in terms of cardiovascular fitness. A major career change, which occurred just at that time, conspired against this, however, and this was one ambition that unfortunately got put on the back burner.

Shortly after I had attended the Prep Course at Bisham, an interesting job was advertised in the *Times Educational Supplement*. This was for a one-year appointment as a lecturer in physical education and sport at Carnegie, which was part of Leeds Polytechnic. Carnegie had originally been one of the top male specialist PE colleges in England (the male equivalent of Dartford). It was now co-ed and still a highly prestigious institution. They were looking for someone with a particular expertise in netball, to teach practical sport and physical education components on the BEd and BA degree programmes and supervise students on their teaching practice in schools.

I was excited by the idea of moving into higher education and although it was only a temporary post, I thought that it might give me a foot in the door and perhaps lead to something more permanent. It would be a big change to move away from all my friends and family in the south of England and go all the way up north to teach in Leeds. I really fancied the job, however, so I decided to apply.

I think that it was a combination of my netball and football expertise that helped me to secure the post, which proved to be the springboard for what has been to date a twenty-two-year career as a lecturer in higher education. As a netball player I had represented Kent and Wales. I had also taught curriculum netball and coached successful teams for five years at the Hundred of Hoo School. As they were specifically looking for a netballer, this was probably the aspect of my sporting pedigree that was the most crucial.

My football background did come in useful, however. The England women's team manager, Tommy Tranter, was one of my referees. He was also a lecturer in PE at Borough Road (another top PE college). I think that he knew the Head of PE at Carnegie, Clive Bond, in some capacity. After I was offered and had accepted the job, Clive Bond told me that my reference from Tommy had been a good one and that he had spoken very highly of my ability as a football coach.

There was a lot of detailed planning to do, to be ready to move up from school teaching to college lecturing. I knew that if I was to make a good impression at Carnegie, in the coming year, I would not have any spare time to devote to further coaching qualifications. This was the main reason that my application to take the FA Full Badge was put on hold.

CARNEGIE SCHOOL OF PHYSICAL EDUCATION AND SPORT, LEEDS POLYTECHNIC, 1981/82 & 1983/84

I was to spend two separate years lecturing on a temporary contract at Carnegie, with a year's gap in between when I went to study for a Master's degree. Most of my work at Carnegie revolved around the teaching of sports such as netball, tennis, badminton and volleyball, rather than football, however. This may have reflected the fact that I was the only female lecturer employed to teach games in a predominantly male department.

In terms of team coaching, as I was employed first and foremost for my net-ball ability, I took on the coaching of the college first team and took them to the final of the British Colleges Netball Championships, at Lilleshall National Sports Centre, in 1982. I did put on some recreational football coaching ses-sions for the Carnegie women, but as yet there was no inter-collegiate women's football championship in England for them to enter.

I did, however, have an interesting experience connected to football while I was in my first year of lecturing at Carnegie. The BBC approached me to take part in an Open University programme, which was looking at the whole issue of equal opportunities for women in sport. They came to Carnegie to film me taking a football coaching session with women students and to inter-view me about my experiences as a female who had been involved in both physical education and football. In the programme I talk about the barriers to female participation in football that I had come up against in the school set-ting, both as a pupil and as a teacher, and the more positive climate that I was experiencing at Carnegie, where all the practical PE lectures took place in mixed-sex groups.

Looking back at that programme again now, the views expressed by Ted Croker, the FA secretary, reveal a lot about the FA's attitude to women's football in the early 1980s. At the time the FA did not allow mixed football, even under the age of eleven. In 1978 there had been a high-profile court case after twelve-year-old Theresa Bennett was banned by the FA from playing football for a boys' team in a local league. The Equal Opportunities Commission had supported Theresa in her fight to play, but the FA had won the case on appeal. The decisive factor was a clause in the Sex Discrimination Act of 1975, which made an exemption for competitive sports where physical differences are liable to put one sex at a disadvantage. In the programme the interviewer asks Ted Croker what the physical differences are between males and females that underpinned the court ruling. He replies:

It is a question of ability. It is easy to see that boys tend to be better than girls. It is just one of those physical facts. Football is essentially a physical contact game, a very hard physical contact game. It's very hard to say to boys 'now, don't forget you're playing against girls today so we want you to be a bit more gentle.'

But Theresa Bennett had apparently been one of the strongest and best players in her team! She had received a lot of media support at the time, but it was not until 1991 that the ban on girls playing mixed competitive football (but only under the age of eleven and in schools) was lifted.

On the same issue of physical differences, Ted Croker goes on to comment:

It has been said that with a bit of luck, most women are not really made for football and whether that is true, I don't know. But I think that adult women are certainly limited in what they can do. For instance, bringing a ball under control is one of the most important aspects of football, and one type of control that men use repeatedly is of course using their chest. Now I don't think that this would be healthy for women to do this.

This particular old chestnut (if you'll pardon the pun) was always being used in the early days as an argument against women playing football. Eric Worthington, the first England women's team manager, apparently used to say that women's chests made a natural trap, which actually gave them an advantage over men in this department!

The programme went on to look at what the FA was doing to support women's football in England at that time. Ted Croker tells the interviewer:

We encourage women's football to a limited extent. We give support to the WFA and in the game generally women are far more involved than they used to be. There are a lot of female secretaries now at clubs and women referees in junior football. We give a certain amount of support to the ladies. We are still having to look very carefully at to what extent they should be affiliated to football in this country, through the Football Association.

The FA did finally invite the WFA to affiliate, on the same basis as a county FA, a few years later, in 1983. From this point the FA then gave the WFA a small grant to assist with the running of the sport. I think that the BBC paid me about £25 for my contribution to that *Women in Sport* programme, which, at the time, I was quite pleased with. After it had been shown twice every year, right up until 1987, it didn't seem to be such good value!

I had a great two years at Carnegie and, after leaving in 1984, I lectured for two years in the PE Department at De La Salle College, near Manchester. As the only female in the Department, I was once again assigned to teach the traditionally female sports, such as netball, hockey, badminton and gymnastics. I didn't really get the chance to get back into football until I secured a post at Chester College of Higher Education (now known as University College Chester) in 1987.

CHESTER COLLEGE OF HIGHER EDUCATION WOMEN'S FOOTBALL TEAM, 1987-1989

I took up my appointment as a lecturer in physical education and sports science at the college in January 1987. I was pleased to discover that there was already a women's football club in existence, although it was operating at a purely recreational level. The students were playing friendly matches against any opposition that they could find, as there was still no organised inter-collegiate women's football. They were involved mainly for social reasons and as a relaxation from the more serious pursuit of their other main college sports (quite a few of the football team were, for instance, also first-team hockey and netball players).

So here we were, over ten years on from the time that I had coached my first college women's football team at Dartford and the sport had still not really gained a proper foothold in the Higher Education sector. Women's football in this country was still firmly located in the voluntary sector (where it had begun its renaissance in the late 1960s and early 1970s). Had I been lecturing in the USA, instead of England, at the time, I would have seen a totally different picture; the college system was proving to be the cradle of the rapidly growing sport over there.

I can't remember who approached whom, but by the following September (1987) I was coaching the college's women's football team and we had entered the local women's league to ensure that we had regular fixtures and a goal to aim for. In order to get the team into shape for league competition, I agreed to take the regular weekly training sessions to give them more structure and progression. Prior to my involvement the players had just turned up for a kickabout among themselves. I soon discovered that the squad, although small and previously uncoached, contained a nucleus of really good players. These included Donna Jones, Paula Gidman and Shiobhan Murphy (who were a formidable midfield trio), Jessica Gamain and Jackie Waller (stalwarts in defence) and Fiona Miley (a skilful winger). In Fiona, we had what Sven-Goran Eriksson can only dream about, a left winger with a natural left foot. She regularly whipped in excellent crosses for our talented centre forward Fiona Wilson to finish off.

These seven players formed the basis of what was to become a very strong team. Our problem was that we were always struggling to make up the numbers for a full squad. For every match, we had to bring in several ringers who were often complete newcomers to the game. This did lead to some amusing incidents, however. A case in point was the time that we had a novice goalkeeper playing for us. In attempting to drop-kick the ball upfield, she somehow managed to kick the ball backwards over her head towards our goal. It took an extremely timely goal-line clearance from our centre-back Jessica Gamain to save the day!

In our first season in the league we soon found that there was a real disparity in the age range and quality of the teams. We won quite a few matches just because we were playing against women who were older and less fit than a team of college students who were all studying PE. In other games we were on the losing side because we came up against women in their late twenties and early thirties who were physically much stronger than us. The problem was that due to the relatively small number of girls and women that were playing the sport in England at that time, the league teams were all open age and mixed ability. Consequently you had thirteen-year-old girls playing against thirty-year-olds and technically competent players competing against virtual beginners. This did make the risk of injury much greater than has been the case since junior age group teams and a meritocratic league structure have been put in place.

The perceived risk of injury to female students from playing football was something that the coaches of other sports teams in the college were apparently concerned about at the time. Fiona Miley recalls her first-team hockey coach being slightly disapproving of her playing football for this reason.

Student members of the other clubs regarded women's football as a bit of a novelty. The men's football team initially came to watch the women's games out of curiosity, not because they were serious spectators. This did all start to change however. In our second season in the league, the team was beginning to play really well, achieve good results and attract an appreciative crowd. Unfortunately just as we were moving in the right direction, things started to unravel.

Being the only college side in the local women's league presented similar problems to those that I had experienced when coaching the Dartford College team in the 1970s. Basically what we came up against was a cultural divide. Because our team was different and made up entirely of students, some of the other clubs seemed to be very wary of us. We got the impression that they came to play against us with the express intention of 'roughing us up a bit'. This escalated to the point that some of our girls felt extremely intimidated and didn't want to compete in the league (some of them actually became disillusioned with football altogether). We discussed the situation together as a club and decided that it would be in the best interests of the players and the future of the sport in the college to pull out of the league and go back to playing friendly matches instead.

As time went on, however, we struggled to find opponents and in the absence of regular fixtures, it became difficult to motivate the players to turn up to practice. What we really needed was a British Colleges competition to enter but, in the absence of that, the college women's football team folded for a while. The club was to be re-established in the mid to late 1990s, by which time college and university sport had amalgamated under one association (BUSA) and the women's football team had been able to enter the BUSA Women's football championships.

Although the experience had been relatively short-lived, coaching that very first Chester College women's team was very rewarding and helped me to settle in to the college. It was great to work with such a talented group of players who enjoyed both their football and the social side of the sport. Training was lively but the atmosphere was always relaxed, which is something that the players have told me that they appreciated.

I was pleased to learn recently that several members of the team had continued with their involvement in football after leaving college. Fiona Miley and Jackie Waller, for instance, both went on to play for Oldham Athletic in the North-West Regional League. They also trained as coaches, passed the FA Coaching Certificate and coached in England and abroad. Jackie became a primary school teacher and taught the game to young girls at her school. Fiona Miley undertook important development work in girls' and women's football as a sports development officer employed by Manchester City Council and later as one of the first female football development officers to work for the Manchester FA. I bumped into Fiona again, in 1997, at an FA conference. She was there to receive a prestigious award for innovation in girls' and women's football, for a floodlit schools' football league for under-twelve, under-fourteen and under-sixteen-year-old girls that she had set-up and run in Manchester.

So, although the first Chester College of Higher Education Women's football team had only run for a few seasons, our efforts had not been wasted. We had thrown a stone into the water and the ripples were still travelling outwards!

seven

A New Era

In 1993, the FA finally took over the running of women's football in this country. This had been a long time coming (in most of the leading European women's football nations the game has been run by the national football association since the 1970s). The WFA had done a great job of rejuvenating women's football in England during the 1970s and 1980s but by the early 1990s, as a voluntary organisation, with limited resources, it found itself struggling to keep pace with the demands of a sport that was growing in popularity. When the FA took over the reigns in July 1993, it signalled the start of a new era for women's football in England.

The impact of this development wasn't immediately felt, however. The real boost to the women's game came in 1997, when the FA put a development strategy for girls' and women's football into place that resulted in the implementation of a number of initiatives, designed to boost both grass-roots participation and elite performance.[1] Kelly Simmons was made head of women's football at that time and over the next few years was to become a real driving force for the game within the FA. The person that I was to have the most contact with, however, was Rachel Pavlou, who was appointed as regional development manager for women's football for the North-West and West Midlands. I was impressed by Rachel's enthusiasm and energy when she came to Cheshire to help the County FA come up with a three-year development plan for girls' football. I was invited to be on the Steering Group responsible for producing it.

Cheshire's plan was approved in 1998 and included a number of initiatives that were indicative of what was being put in place countrywide at that time. One of the main nuts that we felt we had to crack was getting more girls' football into schools. Historically, opportunities for girls to play in schools had been very limited. Despite the best efforts of the WFA in the 1970s and early 1980s it was not until 1991, for instance, that The English Schools

Football Association had changed its constitution to bring schoolgirl football under its remit.

The proposals aimed at developing girls' football in Cheshire schools were to offer fun/taster sessions, set up after-school clubs and provide teacher training in football for female teachers at both primary and secondary levels. In order to then provide a route into clubs, the intention was to support the existing Cheshire Girls' League and help new clubs to get started, by giving help and advice. A number of women-only FA Junior Team Managers courses were also to be put on, at a subsidised cost.[2]

Jacci Cooper from Stockport was appointed as the Cheshire girls' and women's football development officer responsible for putting this plan into action but she was only employed part-time! Like many other dedicated women in football, she worked well over her scheduled hours to ensure its success. By the end of the three years girls' participation in Cheshire had risen dramatically, which was indicative of what was happening nationwide.

The new FA Talent Development Plan for Women's Football was also launched in 1997, via a number of roadshows. I attended the North-West event, which took place at Bolton's Reebok Stadium in their very swish conference facilities. The speakers included Kelly Simmons and some of the FA regional development managers, who were all female. My impressions of the management team were that they were a group of very capable young women, who had good ideas, dynamic personalities, slick presentation skills and a phenomenal capacity for hard work. They outlined their vision for the future with infectious enthusiasm.

The crux of the plan for identifying and developing the talented players of the future was to set up a number of Centres of Excellence for girls' aged ten to sixteen, where they could access quality coaching and sports science support. These would act as feeders for the proposed England youth teams that would in turn link through to the senior side. At the pinnacle of this structure a full-time national coach was to be appointed with responsibility for all the national teams. These initiatives were great news for the development of women's football in this country and something that I personally had been hoping to see for a long time. Now that things were really happening at last I was very keen to play my part.

FA CENTRE OF EXCELLENCE FOR GIRLS' FOOTBALL: TRANMERE
ROVERS FC, 1999-2001

The first twenty FA Centres of Excellence were launched in 1998 and linked to professional clubs. One of these was Tranmere Rovers FC on the Wirral, which is not that far from Chester. In 1999, I got a call from my ex-England colleague Sylvia Gore, who had been appointed as the centre co-ordinator. Since retiring as a player Sylvia had maintained her involvement in the game. She had coached the Welsh national team for seven years before becoming a voluntary football development officer in Liverpool and Preston. The centre was about to go into its second season of operation (1999/2000) and Sylvia was ringing to ask if I would like to come and take charge of the coaching for the under-sixteens. As this was just the sort of opportunity that I had been looking for, I readily agreed to take on the role.

The centre offered a select group of under-twelve, under-fourteen and under-sixteen-year-old girls the opportunity to experience quality coaching for one-and-a-half hours a week over a twenty-week period. The climax of the programme was a Centre of Excellence Festival held at Warwick University, where England scouts came to watch the teams from all over the country play against each other in friendly competition.

Graham Smith was the director and 'A' Licence coach at Tranmere when I was working there. He had been the football development officer at Everton FC and was now lecturing at Edge Hill University. Graham's role was to plan and oversee the centre's coaching programme and mentor the other coaches. He had just the right approach to the job. Always upbeat and chatty with every-one, he had a great sense of humour, which motivated those around him, both players and coaches. As well as ensuring that the programme was running smoothly, Graham also used to move around the age groups, taking the occa-sional demonstration session. I found this very useful and picked up some good ideas from Graham over the two years that I worked at the centre.

The other female coach involved was Louise Edwards, who worked with the under-twelves. Louise was employed at Tranmere Rovers FC on the Community Development programme. At the time she played football for Tranmere Rovers Ladies in the FA Women's Premier League and she has since become the manager of the team.

The players at the centre were drawn from the junior sections of a range of women's clubs in the area, including Everton, Liverpool, Tranmere Rovers and Manchester United. The establishment of junior teams had been a fairly recent and crucial development in the women's game. Before that, competi-tion had been open age and young girls would find themselves having to play with and against mature women. This had certainly been a problem in my playing days. Everton, for instance, now have teams at the following levels: under-tens, twelves, fourteens, sixteens, reserves and Women's Premier League, which is typical of a lot of top women's clubs and can only be good for the future of the game.

Coaching at the centre proved to be a rewarding experience. It was great to work with better players and see them progress. Most of the girls were very appreciative of the chance to be there and worked hard, although some of the players who had already been selected for the England Under-16 team could be rather difficult to motivate at times.

Taking the team to the Centre of Excellence tournament at Warwick was a highlight. The set-up was fantastic. The university had extensive fields that were all marked out with football pitches. All the centres from around the country were there, most bringing teams from the three age groups. That represented a large number of talented young girls who were getting a really good competitive experience as well as a great day out. I couldn't help being mildly jealous that nothing comparable had been available at that level in my playing days! As I was wandering around to have a look at some of the competition on the other pitches, I was surprised to bump into another of my ex-England colleagues, Sue Lopez. Sue had played for the mighty Southampton Ladies back in the 1970s. Here was another player from my era who had stayed involved and put a lot back into the game (as far as I am aware there are not that many of us). An excellent coach, she was one of the first women in England to be awarded the 'A' Licence in the early 1990s. Sue was, at the time, working in a full-time capacity for Hampshire FA. She has since gone on to become head of women's football at Southampton Football Club and in 2000 was awarded an MBE for her services to the sport. At the Warwick tournament she was acting as an FA scout, looking for new talent to join the England Under-16 squad. It was good to know that someone with Sue's pedigree was involved in the talent identification process at the national level.

As a feeder for the England youth sides, the Tranmere Rovers Centre of Excellence was to be very successful over the coming years. Everton player Kelly McDougall, who was in my under-sixteen squad, has gone on to play for England Under-21s and the full England team. Fern Whelan and Claire Owen have both played for the Under-17s while Fay Dunne, Jody Taylor, Michelle Evans and Heather Scheuber have all represented England at Under-19 level. Kelly Leyland, meanwhile, has played for Northern Ireland.

As centre co-ordinator for the last seven years Sylvia Gore has seen all these players pass through. She has given years of valuable service to women's football, mostly in a voluntary capacity, a fact that was recognised and rewarded in the year 2000 when Sylvia received both a prestigious UEFA award and the MBE.

AXA COACHING DAY WITH MICHAEL OWEN AND EMILE HESKEY:
CHESTER CITY FC, 2001

One of the spin-offs of being involved with Sylvia Gore at Tranmere was that she contacted me when she was looking for coaches to staff a coaching day for AXA employees at Chester City FC. The event was a competition prize. The winners would spend a day at the club, where they would have the opportunity to meet and talk with Michael Owen and Emile Heskey, then both playing for Liverpool FC, and take part in some football coaching sessions. AXA were, at the time, the sponsors of the men's FA Cup competition, although the day was not connected to that in any way.

I was very excited at the idea of taking part, not least because it meant that we (the coaches) would have the chance to meet the Liverpool players in the boardroom before the start of the event. We were to discuss the role that they wanted to play in the coaching sessions during the afternoon and have our own private photograph session with them.

There were two other coaches that I would be working with on the day: Jacci Cooper from the Cheshire FA and Louise Edwards from Tranmere Rovers. We were all in the Chester City boardroom, together with Sylvia Gore and the AXA organisers, waiting expectantly for Michael and Emile to arrive. The first thing that struck me when Emile Heskey walked through the door was how much smaller he looked in person than on the television. He was tall and athletic-looking, but not nearly as bulky in the upper body as the television cameras make him appear. Both he and Michael Owen seemed quite shy and reserved in the face of a room full of people to whom they had suddenly become the focus of attention.

The AXA officials quickly moved to welcome them and introduced them to everyone else. At that point I was able to speak briefly to both players and have my photograph taken with them. They also did a signing session of various items such as shirts, shorts and photographs that had been laid out on a table for the purpose.

The programme for the day was then outlined. Michael and Emile were to spend the next hour or so talking to the competition winners and signing autographs, before coming out on to the pitch to observe the coaching sessions. I was really excited but very nervous to discover that Michael Owen was to be assigned to my coaching group for the afternoon. I was already apprehensive because Jacci Cooper and I had been asked to plan an afternoon's coaching without having any prior information about the age or standard of the group. Given these constraints, making a good job of delivering it, under the watchful eye of Michael Owen, was going to be a challenge!

In the final analysis I think that we put on a pretty good session, which the players seemed to enjoy. We did ask Michael at one point if he would like to be involved in the coaching but he was more than happy for us to get on with things, while he observed from the sidelines. Once we had got the group into a final five-a-side game, I took the opportunity to go over and chat with him. We watched the game together for a while and I asked him for his thoughts on how the players were performing. I was quite pleased with them because the session had been on passing and both teams were keeping possession well when they had the ball. Michael, however, as you might expect was watching proceedings with his striker's hat on. He was quite right when he said, 'The passing is quite good but there is no penetration. Neither team has looked like scoring yet.' I stopped the game, brought the group over and invited Michael to give them some tips on looking for the final penetrating pass. Apart from anything else I knew that the players would really want to be able to go away from the day and tell their friends that they had been given some advice on how to score goals by Michael Owen!

What my friends wanted to know afterwards was what Michael Owen was like. Although I had only spent a relatively short time in his company that afternoon, I had been very impressed by what I saw. I told them that he had come across as a really polite, unassuming young man, who did not appear to have been affected by his celebrity. Chatting to Michael had, in fact, felt no different to talking to one of my students, to whom he was very close in age anyway.

The big age gap between myself and Michael was not something that I had thought about on the day, but it was brought home to me when I went to collect my photographs from the local camera shop. On reading my name (Wendy Owen) on the redemption slip and seeing the photograph of Michael and I together, the man in the shop asked me if I was Michael Owen's mother!

UEFA COACHING AWARDS, 1998-2001

Inspired by the FA's new-found commitment towards the development of women's football in England, I had decided to finally have a go at taking the 'A' Licence coaching award. When I looked into this, however, I discovered that the goalposts had shifted. The FA had recently restructured its award scheme to embrace the UEFA qualifications. There was now an interim award between the FA Coaching Certificate and the 'A' Licence, which was called the UEFA 'B' Licence. I would have to pass this before I was eligible to apply for the 'A' Licence. All this was going to require a big commitment in terms of time and energy, over several years. I must have been mad at the time because I decided to give it a go!

UEFA 'B' LICENCE, 1998-99

I began this process in September 1998, the year before I began coaching at Tranmere Rovers, when I enrolled on a UEFA 'B' Licence course with Lancashire FA. The new FA coaching courses turned out to be far more demanding than those that I had taken previously. As well as attending a rigorous one-week taught course at Leyland, in Lancashire, in the September, I then had to go away and do regular coaching sessions in the community, keeping a logbook of all my planning and evaluations. There were additional tasks for the 'B' Licence related to fitness, sports psychology and match analysis. After all this had been completed, candidates had to present themselves for an interview and final practical coaching assessment.

The 1998/99 academic year was going to be a very busy one indeed. I had all the responsibilities of my full-time lecturing post at Chester College of Higher Education to contend with, plus the theoretical and practical work associated with a Level 3 FA Coaching award. The coaching experience required for the UEFA 'B' Licence needed to be at a fairly high standard of play, due to the complexity of the topics and coaching scenarios involved in this level of award. In order to meet these requirements, I approached the college's men's football club, to see if they needed any help in the forthcoming season. They were more than happy to have a lecturer in the PE and Sports Science Department on board and I became coach to the first team for what was to be a two-year spell between 1998 and 2000.

I was a little apprehensive at the very beginning because although I had coached a male team in the past, this had been at school level. The men's first team was in the top division of the BUSA North-West Conference at the time and had players in the team like Ben Fuller, who played representative football for North-West Universities and later went on to play in the FA Cup with Chelmsford City. I did have the benefit of the fact that I already taught most of the players on coaching modules as part of their PE and Sports Science degree and could therefore command some sort of respect as one of their lecturers. I knew, however, that this would only take me so far. If I didn't make a good job of things on the training ground then this would soon count for nothing.

As part of the requirements for the UEFA 'B' Licence I had to do some video analysis of the team's performance over a number of games. This was before the college acquired its performance analysis laboratory and hi-tech computer analysis equipment. I had to resort to the laborious process of playing back the footage on my home video recorder using its very unsophisticated pause and freeze-frame facility. This took me hours but it did pay off. I was able to identify areas of weakness that the team needed to work on (most of them were actually pretty obvious to me with the naked eye anyway!) and offer proof of this to the lads.

One of the main problems was that the team was mainly playing long-ball football; every time our goalkeeper got the ball he tried to hit our forwards with it. The video analysis showed that the opposition were winning possession from these kicks on a much higher percentage of occasions than we were and the ball was in effect coming right back at us. There were other aspects that we needed to work on also but this was where I made a start. I did a series of coaching sessions aimed at trying to make the team efficient at playing out from the back, so that defenders and midfield players became confident enough to create space to receive the ball to feet from the goalkeeper. I also worked on playing the ball through the midfield as an option to trying to always give it straight to the forwards, and generally did a lot of possession work with them until we no longer gave the ball away so cheaply.

These sessions all seemed to go down well. Attendance at training was good and the players all seemed to be motivated to work hard for me. In researching this book I spoke to Ryan Willis, who played in the team for the two seasons that I was coach. He captained the side in 1999/2000, which was my second season in charge. He told me that the players enjoyed the coaching sessions that I delivered and respected me as a coach because they knew that I was working on the things that they needed to improve on to become successful as a team.

All the hard work both on and off the field in the 1998/99 season paid off. The Chester College of Higher Education men's team performed well to come fourth in the league and qualify for the Championship Cup competition, and I passed my UEFA 'B' Licence coaching award.

UEFA 'A' LICENCE: 2000-01

At my final interview after my UEFA 'B' Licence practical coaching assessment in 1999, my assessor Graham Keeley indicated to me that, in his opinion, I would be ready to take my 'A' Licence the following year. He duly supported my application and in the summer of 2000 I finally made it on to an 'A' Licence course at Lilleshall National Sports Centre, nearly twenty years after I had received the go ahead from Allen Wade to take the old Full Qualifying Licence! As I said earlier in the book, I shall always regret that I didn't take the award when I was young, fit and still playing competitive football. I think that those qualities would have been great assets to have been able to take with me when I embarked on the course in July 2000!

Two weeks at Lilleshall, as one of only two women in a group of thirty-six candidates, on a residential course staffed entirely by males, turned out to be a really tough test of both physical and mental endurance. It was physically tough for everyone because we spent long days out on the field playing football, followed by theory seminars in the evening. Even the comparatively young male ex-professional players struggled (young compared to a forty-something-year-old woman, that is!).

It was mentally tiring because we had no contact with the outside world for two weeks and for that time were totally immersed in football 24/7. To add to the pressure, on several occasions during the fortnight, each candidate had to deliver a coaching session under the scrutiny of several assessors in the knowledge that a tick in every box on the scoresheet was required in order to succeed!

I managed to get through the course, which included two-week residential stays at Lilleshall in the summers of both 2000 and 2001, mainly due to the fantastic support and camaraderie from the other candidates. All the lads on the course were great fun and would always help you out in a crisis. We had some good ex-professionals in the group including Bobby Mimms, who had played in goal for Tottenham; Perry Suckling, a goalkeeper for Crystal Palace; Nigel Pearson (Sheffield Wednesday) and John Pemberton (Crystal Palace). There was always a lot of playful banter going on between them which was very entertaining. Perry Suckling was often on the receiving end – they used to tease him mercilessly about a game that he had played in against Liverpool, where he had let in nine goals. He was extremely good natured, however, and took it all in good part.

The lads were great but I couldn't have survived without Josie Clifford (née Lee). When I had discovered that Josie was going to be on the course I was really pleased. Josie and I were contemporaries; we knew each other from the 1970s when we had played on opposing teams in the Home Counties League. Josie was an excellent player who had played for QPR (one of the top teams at the time) at the same time that I was playing for Thame. She then went on to play for England, just after I had finished, and gained 5 caps between 1977 and 1979. Since then, Josie had been involved in football coaching and sports development work. It was great to see her again; Josie's lively sense of humour proved to be just what I needed. Although we found ourselves in different coaching groups for the fortnight, we were able to meet up at other times. As the only females on the course, we gave each other moral support. When things got too claustrophobic or we just couldn't stand institutionalised food any more, we would leap into the car, drive off down the Lilleshall country lanes and stop at a restaurant for something different to eat. On one occasion we got really lost and couldn't find our way back. We got back for the 8 p.m. lecture by the skin of our teeth!

Having survived the fortnight at Lilleshall in July/August 2000, we then went away for the year to complete logged coaching sessions, plus various tasks similar to those that we had undertaken for the 'B' Licence. In the summer of 2001, we returned to Lilleshall for another two-week stint that included our final practical and theoretical assessments. At the end of all this hard work, both Josie and I passed all the theoretical components but were referred for further assessment on the practical coaching side. I was very disappointed at the time, but when I discovered later that only one person from our course of thirty-six candidates had passed, I didn't feel quite so bad!

The 'A' Licence course is a very demanding one and rightly so. Judging by my own personal experience, however, I would say that for a woman (struggling not to let herself and other women down, as one of the few female candidates on a predominantly male course) it is doubly difficult. The FA has now introduced a mentoring programme for female coaches who are working towards the 'A' Licence, which should help. In my opinion it would also be really beneficial if at some point in the future, when there are enough female candidates to do so, the FA could run a women-only 'A' Licence course, as they have done in the past for the Preliminary Coaching Certificate. Getting more female tutors involved in the delivery of 'A' Licence courses would also, in my opinion, be desirable. In 2000 there were only seven 'A' Licence female coaches in England, compared to 1,105 males.[3] I am sure that measures like those suggested above could really help to give a much needed boost to the number of qualified female coaches at the top end of the coaching ladder in this country.

SPORT CHESHIRE ADVANCED COACHING CENTRE FOR GIRLS' FOOTBALL: UNIVERSITY COLLEGE CHESTER, 2002-04

Having spent two years as coach to the under-sixteen girls at Tranmere Rovers' Centre of Excellence between 1999 and 2001, I became interested in the idea of setting up a similar centre at University College Chester (the title given to the college after its change of status in August 2003). As well as being more accessible to local girls, it would also provide coach-development opportunities for my female students. I approached Cheshire FA to see if there was any way of linking this in with the FA Talent Development Programme.

My timing was just right. Cheshire FA informed me that the Sport Cheshire Active Sports Partnership (of which they were a part) was looking to set up a third Advanced Coaching Centre for Girls' Football, in 2002/03, to complement the existing centres at Stockport and Crewe. Funded as part of a five-year (2000-2005) Active Sports programme (a partnership project between Sport England, the FA and the Football Foundation, which has put £8 million of funding into women's football[4]) these centres were to provide coaching for under-twelve and under-fourteen development squads and act as feeders for the Centre of Excellence at Tranmere.

The advanced coaching centre at the college started in October 2002 with me as director and ran for two seasons. In that time it made a real contribution to the development of girls' and women's football on a number of fronts. Each year approximately thirty-two talented young girls from the local area, including players from Chester, Ellesmere Port, Warrington and surrounding areas, received a twenty-week programme from qualified coaches, covering all the basic skills of the game. Each group (under-twelves and under-fourteens) had at least one female coach working with it. In me, the players also had a centre director who was female and had played football for England. In terms of providing the girls with positive female role models, something that historically had not been available to young girls who were trying to get involved in football in this country, you would have to say that the centre scored highly.

From the participants' point of view, their experience certainly appeared to have been a positive one. Feedback questionnaires, filled in by each girl at the end of the season, showed that the majority had enjoyed being taught new skills by friendly coaches in a well-organised and spacious environment. From a coach education standpoint, the venture had also been a success. Over the two seasons, the centre employed five female coaches (Jo Bullen, Mary Guilfoyle, Kym Gaskell, Sarah Burnyeat and Sylvia Eager) who were all members of the University College Chester Women's Football club (a club that I had been involved with as first-team coach since 2000). They all received mentoring from me, in terms of assistance with planning and evaluative feedback. Some also gained further, subsidised coaching qualifications as a result of their employment as an active sports coach. These women have subsequently gone out into the community (at least one has become a PE teacher) to work in schools and clubs, where they will hopefully introduce football to the next generation of girls.

From my point of view, the centre had been very worthwhile. It was great to be able to offer the kind of opportunities to female players and coaches that had not been available to me in my early career in football. To see girls as young as ten, who already had great skills and a wonderful enthusiasm for the game, blossom under the guidance of some very capable student coaches, was a very rewarding experience. I had put a lot of time and energy into the centre, both in terms of setting it up, organising and supporting the coaches and being there every week, come rain or shine, to oversee its smooth running. It was a great disappointment to me therefore when the FA decided, in 2004, to stop funding the advanced coaching centres and take them out of the talent development continuum, although I can appreciate its reasons for doing so.

In researching this book, I spoke to Kelly Simmons who is now the head of national football development at the FA, a very prestigious post that she took up in 2000. She told me that they took the tough decision to dispense with the advanced coaching centres in order to redirect funds to the centres of excellence. These were in need of greater investment to allow a programme of competitive fixtures with other centres to be developed. Rather than spreading the funding thinly across a two-tier elite player development structure, it was felt that it would be better to properly resource one.

Having coached at the Centre of Excellence at Tranmere Rovers, I can appreciate the need for competitive fixtures. The absence of these was certainly a real problem in terms of both motivating the girls to stay with the programme and measuring and developing their performance. The advanced coaching centres did, however, give more girls at the top end of the football continuum an opportunity to access quality coaching and while the centre at Chester was in operation, Sylvia Gore at Tranmere Rovers was able to send girls who didn't quite make the grade down to me for further development and I could send girls that had sufficiently improved up to her. This seemed to work very well and it is a shame that this link has now been lost.

COACHING THE CHESTER COLLEGE/UNIVERSITY COLLEGE CHESTER WOMEN'S FOOTBALL TEAM, 2000-2004

At the same time that I was running the Sport Cheshire Advanced Coaching Centre, I was also coaching the college women's football team. When I began working with them in October 2000 they were already an established club. The set-up was very different to the one that I had experienced when I had last worked with a Chester women's team back in 1989. This was indicative of both the growth in popularity of football among females in the interim and the progress that had at last been made in establishing the game in Britain as a competitive inter-collegiate sport.

The original Chester College of Higher Education Women's Football Club had struggled to find both players and opponents. When I turned up to the first training session of the 2000/01 season I was delighted to find a squad of about thirty players who were keen and ready to tackle their forthcoming fixtures in the BUSA (British Universities Sports Association) Women's eleven-a-side Football Championship. With that number of players we were able to run two teams, entering the second team in to the BUSA competition from the following season.

Since the competition's inception in the 1988/89 season, when sixteen universities took part, the number of teams participating had grown considerably. During my first season as coach in the new era for women's football at the college, the team was competing in tier two of the Northern Conference in an overall structure that boasted 101 teams.[5]

This was to be the beginning of four very enjoyable seasons of coaching for me, during which time I was fortunate to be able to work with a great bunch of players. There was plenty of talent in the squad but also some great characters who managed to strike the perfect balance between hard work on the pitch and having a great time off it! The players took the game very seriously and were first and foremost football players, rather than hockey or netball players who were playing football as a second sport. This was again one of the big differences between this college women's football squad and those that I had worked with in the past. The squad trained three times a week at their sport and played matches on a Wednesday.

One of the most gifted players in the squad was Geraldine (Ger) Lynch, who played for the first team between 2000 and 2003, captaining the side in

2001/02. She was a mature student from Dublin, who had played Premier League football in Ireland and represented Irish Universities before coming over to England to study PE and Sports Science at Chester. She was a brilliant midfield player, with fantastic ball skills, and was good enough to have played in a full international side.

Ger was one of a strong contingent of Irish players that the first team was able to call upon over the years. Others included Aideen McCann, Jennifer Leitch, Fiona Ryan and Sylvia Eager. Aideen was club captain in my first season as coach (2000/01). She was one of many natural leaders who had a big influence over the years both on and off the field. Others included club and first-team captains Jenny Clews, Emma Dawson, Jenny Leitch, Geraldine Lynch, Sarah Burnyeat and Jo Bullen; social secretaries Lisa Cahalan, Lucy Bailes, Fiona Ryan and Mary Guilfoyle; and players like Sally Stewart and Gobi Sherwood. Between them they ensured that there were no cliques in the club and that everyone (all year groups and both first and second-team players) mixed together.

The social secretaries were a very important part of the club's set-up and were very inventive in coming up with different themes for the squad's entertainment. Playing together on and off the field was very important and helped to build a cohesive team unit. I didn't usually get involved on these occasions but I did make an exception at the end-of-season celebrations when I ran a karaoke night after the awards ceremony. This provided me with the opportunity to dust off those Elvis numbers that I had entertained the England team with back in the 1970s during my playing days!

The great sense of camaraderie between everyone at the club (players and coaching staff) was probably one of its greatest assets and definitely played a part in our successes in BUSA competition. The first team were champions of tier two in the Northern Conference in 2000/01 and 2001/02, competed in tier one from 2002-04 and were placed third in that division on both occasions. The team also reached the semi-finals of the Shield Competition for two seasons in a row between 2001 and 2003. We may not have been able to match the achievements of large universities like Loughborough, who have won the competition no less than eight times since 1988, and Bath, who were runners-up to Loughborough in the finals of 2003 and 2004, but for a college of higher education these were good achievements and contributed to the women's football club being named 'club of the year', a title bestowed by the student's union, for three years in a row between 2000 and 2003.

I will particularly remember that group of players (I apologise to all those that there has not been the space to mention) not only for their football skills but the laughs that they gave me at training and their friendship outside the coaching environment. One of the great characters in the squad during those years was Fiona Ryan. She was one player who often had me in stitches at training because she could never seem to grasp what I was trying to put over. On one occasion I was trying to teach her (as a forward) how to spin in behind a defender. Try as I might she kept spinning the wrong way, right into the defender. I must have demonstrated four or five times before her housemate Ger Lynch said, 'leave it and carry on Wendy, we'll be here all night. I'll teach her when we get home.' Ger then apparently got Fiona to practise in the kitchen, spinning from the cooker to the kitchen table with a chair in the way so that she could practice spinning away from the chair. The next week she executed the move perfectly in a match and the rest of the team stopped in their tracks and couldn't play for laughing!

Hopefully I made some impression on the players over the years, if only to give them a female role model. In researching this book I did speak to several of the players who told me that they were motivated by the fact that they had a coach who had played for England and coached at a good level.

The club has produced some good coaches of its own over the years. Jenny Clews and Kym Gaskell were the two most highly qualified. They both came to college with the Preliminary Coaching Certificate already under their belts. Jenny went over to the USA to coach in the summer vacation while she was at college and Kym has worked at the Advanced Coaching Centre at Chester College and for Cheshire FA. Natalie Slack, Jo Bullen and Mary Guilfoyle all took their Level 1 Coaching Award with me while they were at Chester and, together with Ger Lynch, went to the USA for a while to coach soccer for UK Elite. Sylvia Eager and Sarah Burnyeat also gained their Level 1 Certificates and assisted with the coaching at the advanced coaching centre.

Quite a few members of the women's football squad have gone on to become PE teachers in recent years, including Jenny Clews, Jenny Leitch, Natalie Slack, Aideen McCann, Mary Guilfoyle and Geraldine Lynch. I am sure that wherever they are now, they will be seizing the opportunity to spread the word!

Having coached various college women's football teams over the last thirty years, I would have to say that the speed of the development of the game in the Higher Education (HE) Sector has been painfully slow. It took a very long time for an inter-collegiate tournament to get off the ground and when it did the number of teams in it was very low. The FA did put some money in during the mid-1990s in the form of grant aid to colleges to assist them in paying for the services of an FA-qualified coach to help develop a women's team. When this was deemed to have been a success (when the number of teams entering the BUSA Women's Championship had grown by the end of the 1990s to nearly 100 teams) this funding was switched into the Further Education (FE) sector to be used for the same purpose.[6] The FA has continued to work with BUSA and helped the organisation to get some funding through the FA Youth Trust. The amount per year is fairly small, however, (about £25,000) and has to help support the BUSA competition structures for men's and women's football and the England Universities men's and women's teams.

In researching this book, I spoke to Donna McIvor, who is national development manager (education) at the FA. She told me that elite women's football in higher education is not really an FA priority. She was of the opinion that the talent pool at the elite end of the game is not big enough at the moment to support it. The efforts of her department are currently being directed into FE rather than HE, where they are reviewing the FA Academies for sixteen to nineteen-year-olds. These were set up as partnerships between colleges and professional clubs to extend the excellence programme post-sixteen and enable talented players to receive coaching alongside their academic studies. The FA now apparently wants to see the academies driven more through the professional clubs and linked more closely to the centres of excellence, which appears to be in keeping with the predominantly club-based approach to elite sport development that has been the norm in this country for many years. This is very different to the college-based approach that has been adopted in the USA. Personally, I think that Higher Education could be a rich breeding ground for elite female football players and coaches in this country and is a sector that is ripe for further development.

WORKING AS A COACH EDUCATOR

Since gaining my UEFA 'B' Licence in 1999, I have gone on to attend a number of FA tutor training courses and qualified as an FA Coach Educator. This has enabled me to deliver coaching award courses to University College Chester students and other groups, through the Cheshire FA. Rather than being something that I have only recently been concerned with, however, this is just an extension of the coach-education work that I have been involved in for many years, as a lecturer in physical education and sport.

The coach-education modules that I have delivered on the undergraduate programme at University College Chester over the last ten years have taken me out into the community on a regular basis to mentor student football coaches in a range of schools and clubs, including Chester City Football Club. Most of the students involved have been male, although the number of female coaches has increased in recent years. It would be interesting at this point for me to be able to recount amusing stories about all the quizzical looks and comments that I received from male students and male football club officials as a female coach educator. I can't, however, because I don't have any. As far as I was aware, no one batted an eyelid. It didn't seem to be an issue, which perhaps indicated that attitudes to women in football were changing and society was moving on?

Over the last four or five years in particular, it has been pleasing to witness the growth in the number of female students who have become involved in the game and started to make good progress as coaches. The fact that I have, at the same time, been working with the women's football club has been influential. It has enabled me to get to know the players well, identify those who have an interest in coaching and direct them towards training and coaching opportunities both within and outside the curriculum. Since 2002, for instance, I have been running Level 1 FA Coaching Certificate courses at college and the uptake among females has been good. I am sure that this has had something to do with the fact that they feel more confident to enrol with their teammates on a course tutored by a female who they are already familiar and comfortable with. This is certainly the type of environment that I would have appreciated had it been available to me on the FA Coaching Courses that I have taken in the past.

On the employment front, as well as giving female students the opportunity to gain paid coaching work at the Sport Cheshire Advanced Coaching Centre, I have also developed links with a soccer education company in the USA, called UK Elite, who are based in New Jersey. Every year they employ a number of University College Chester students (both male and female) on work-based learning and summer contracts, to coach soccer to girls and boys ranging from the ages of three to eighteen. Interestingly, this has come about through me re-establishing contact with an ex-student whom I taught at De La Salle between 1984 and 1987. Brendan Doyle was studying PE there at the time. A very talented footballer, he went to play semi-professionally in Spain for a while before going out to the USA to coach for a soccer coaching company. To cut a long story short, he joined another group of Brits, who were all Loughborough University-trained PE teachers as well as soccer coaches, to become a part of UK Elite. The company is so called because they have capitalised on the UK angle. They had a similar experience to the one that I had when I was over in the USA coaching soccer in the 1970s. That is that everyone over there loved their funny accent and thought that because they were English they must know about soccer – which they actually did of course! Initially all their coaches were brought over from the UK and they were able to give the players and the parents a cultural as well as a soccer experience. They still employ a large number of UK coaches.

Because they were teachers as well as coaches, they wanted to blend the two together, which is something that I have always tried to do, and add an educational element to the fun of playing soccer. I have found them to be a good company to send students to work with because of this strong educational philosophy. They give the coaches training when they arrive and follow this up with ongoing observation and feedback sessions. This has mirrored the type of mentoring support that our students have been given on coach-education modules back at college, so it has dovetailed nicely. When they come back, the students have bags of confidence and are full of new ideas.

With women's soccer becoming so big in the USA, the demand for female coaches has increased and a growing number of the University College Chester Women's Football Team have gone out to coach for UK Elite in recent years. They have all brought back stories about the massive popularity of the game among females over there now, and the dedicated approach to training shown by girls from a very young age in the school and club teams that they have worked with. The women's game has become hugely successful in the USA both as a participation sport and in terms of the achievements of the national team. With things now moving in the right direction in England, it will be interesting to see whether or not women's football, under the auspices of the Football Association, can reach similar heights in this country in the future.

eight

Back to the Future

The year 2005 is going to be a particularly important one for the future of women's football in England. In June, we are playing host to the sixth UEFA European Women's Championships, which will take place at various venues in the north-west of England. Seven of the best teams in Europe will be joining the England team (who qualified automatically as hosts) in the finals, for what could be a pivotal moment for the English game. It will be the first time that the FA has staged a major women's championship. If it does a good job and the England team performs well, there is huge potential to propel the sport even further forwards than it has already come.

2005 will also mark thirty-six years of my personal involvement in the women's game. Looking back over my experiences during that time has been an interesting journey. It might at this point be worth reflecting on how far the game has come in that time, where it is now and what the future might hold.

THE PATH OF PROGRESS IN WOMEN'S FOOTBALL IN ENGLAND

So how far have we come?

When I started out in 1969, women had been banned for nearly fifty years from playing on any pitch that came under FA control; in 2005 the current England women's team will be kicking off the UEFA European Championships in the City of Manchester Stadium, home to Manchester City FC. When the WFA was formed, in 1969, to govern the sport in England, there were forty-four registered clubs[1]; by the 2003/04 season, when the sport had been governed by the FA for ten years, there were around 7,000 teams in England, including 1,000 for women and 6,000 for girls.[2] In 1974, there were only five qualified female coaches in this country; in 2000, there were 201 at Preliminary Certificate Level and above.[3] In 1973 (when I set up my first college team at Dartford) there was no inter-collegiate women's football; in the 2003/04 season, 105 teams took part.[4] In 1975, when I participated in the very first international women's football tournament to be staged in this country, there was no television coverage at all. Matches during Euro 2005 will be broadcast live by Eurosport and the BBC. In 1972, when the very first England match took place, there was only one open-age England team and no development programme for promising young players; by 2004, there were England squads at Under-15, Under-17, Under-19, Under-21 and senior levels, a National Player Development Centre, nineteen academies for sixteen to nineteen-year-olds and fifty-one centres of excellence for talented young girls.[5]

Phenomenal progress has obviously been made on all fronts. I would like to think that I have made some small contribution to this, through my efforts both as a player in the early WFA competitions and the first England team and then as a qualified coach and coach educator working within Higher Education and the FA Talent Development Programme.

THE WFA LEGACY

The growth of women's football has accelerated considerably since the FA took over in 1993, when there were only 480 teams in England (400 for women and eighty for girls) and put its weight and resources behind the game. Twenty-four years of hard work by the volunteers at the WFA and the achievements of its England teams should not be forgotten however. Had people like Arthur Hobbs, Patricia Gregory, Flo Bilton, June Jaycocks, David Marlowe and David Hunt not been prepared to dedicate their spare time and energy into developing women's football at a time when no one else was willing to do so, women like myself would have been denied the opportunity to play for club and country and there would have been no national infrastructure or England squad for the FA to build upon.

Due to the skill and dedication of the players and the work of some excellent managers, the record of the England team under the WFA was very impressive. There was no European or World Cup competition to enter when I played for England between 1972 and 1977 but in 18 internationals we won 13, drew 1 and lost 4. The only countries that we lost to were Italy and Sweden. In the first European Competition for Representative Women's teams in 1984, England reached the final, losing on penalties to Sweden. In 1987, we were semi-finalists. Norway went on to win. When this competition was replaced by the UEFA Women's Championships in 1991, England made the quarter-finals, with the eventual winners being Germany. The team was beginning to struggle to keep up with its main European rivals, Germany, Sweden and Norway, however, who had received much better funding and resources at a far earlier stage in their development.

FA INVESTMENT

By the time that the FA eventually took over the running of the women's game in 1993, it was crying out for further investment. This has been forthcoming during recent years and the impact, particularly at the grassroots of the game has been dramatic. Since the start of the Active Sports Programme in 2000, 1,000 new girls' football teams have been formed every year.[6] This is largely the result of work at a county level where women's football development officers have been employed to set up programmes in schools and clubs. In the 2001/02 season, football became the top participation sport for females in England. In 2003/04 the number of females playing the game for registered clubs broke the 100,000 mark.[7]

Provision at the elite end of the game has also improved dramatically. Good players are now identified at the age of ten and nurtured through centres of excellence until the age of sixteen. At this point they can either go on to attend one of the FA academies for sixteen to nineteen-year-olds or, if they are good enough to be selected to represent one of the England youth sides, they can win a fully funded scholarship place at the National Player Development Centre at Loughborough University. This is run by the FA in partnership with the university, Burleigh Specialist Sports College and the Institute of Youth Sport. Sponsored by Umbro, the centre opened its doors to its first intake in the 2001/02 season. The players in the England youth teams (from age sixteen upwards) now live there full time and receive regular quality FA coaching alongside their education, which is provided by the nearby colleges or the university. They are well supported by a team of sports scientists and receive expert advice on nutrition and conditioning. The centre is headed by Jane Ebbage, an 'A' Licence coach, and overseen by Hope Powell, a former England player who was capped 66 times for her country and is now a Pro-Licence Coach, who became the first full-time England women's team coach in 1998. This is a fantastic set-up for England's promising young players and should give them an excellent chance of making the step up to the full England team.

THE ENGLAND TEAM (PAST AND PRESENT)

The experience of playing for the senior England team today is totally different to the one that I enjoyed. In researching this book I compared notes with two of the top players from the current England squad; Faye White, who is England's captain and a central defender, and Kelly Smith, one of England's top strikers. Aged twenty-six (in 2004) they are both very experienced internationals who joined the full England set-up at the tender age of sixteen. Faye had 38 England caps at the time of writing and also captains Arsenal, one of the top club sides in England. Kelly has 39 caps and is the only England player to have played in the women's professional league in the USA (WUSA) where she was with Philadelphia Charge. She has recently returned to the UK to participate in England's Euro 2005 preparations and has signed for Arsenal Ladies.

Faye and Kelly were kind enough to describe the current England set-up to me. The national squad has apparently been getting together for training camps or matches every month for the last three or four years, with on average about eight games being played per year. On these occasions the squad usually meets up on a Sunday and is together through to the following Thursday. Each player receives travelling expenses for their journey to the venue (the FA has paid Kelly Smith's air fares to and from the USA, for instance) and an allowance of up to £400, which compensates for the fact that some players have to take unpaid leave from their work to play for their country. In the build-up to Euro 2005, the England squad will spend six days (in January 2005) at a winter training camp in La Manga, Spain and ten days competing in the Algarve Cup in Portugal (in March). They will also play friendly matches in February, April and May. According to Bev Ward, who is the marketing manager for Women's Football at the FA, this will be the best preparation that an England women's team has ever had before a major tournament.

In contrast, when I played for England in the 1970s we only met up for matches, which were played on average about three times a year, and were lucky if we managed to get together as a squad for more than a day beforehand. We did get some money towards travelling expenses in England, although it didn't always cover the cost. Everything was paid for in terms of accommodation, food and travel while we were away but there was no daily personal allowance given to individuals on top of that and players were often out of pocket for time that they had to take off work. Even so, we thought that we were blessed and taking into account the meagre resources available to the WFA at the time, we were. The WFA's only sources of funding were from players' club subscriptions, a small grant from the Sports Council and an even smaller sum from Mitre Sports, who sponsored the WFA Cup.[8] The FA did fund the England manager's expenses from the outset and later provided a small grant to the WFA. When I was playing for England, however, funding didn't stretch to providing tracksuits for the team, which were either borrowed from the FA for the occasion or provided by the players themselves.

According to Bev Ward, the current England team benefits from a kit sponsorship from Umbro, who produce a specially fitted female shirt, two of which the players are allowed to keep after every match, and a four-year multi-million pound sponsorship package from Nationwide Building Society that was put in place in July 2002. The latter helps to fund the England women's teams and the development squads as well as some of the major national competitions for women, such as the Premier League Cup, the Charity Shield and the FA Cup.

As a result of all this financial input the England women's team currently enjoys vastly improved staffing back-up. When I went on tour with England in the 1970s, we were accompanied by our coach, a physiotherapist, a doctor on away trips and a WFA chaperone, which was in fact very good considering the WFA's limited budget. Today, however, the entourage has expanded considerably. England captain Faye White told me that as well as the head coach (Hope Powell), they have an assistant coach (Brent Hills) and a goalkeeping coach (Keith Rees). In addition to medical back-up and video analysis support, they also have a sports scientist (Dawn Scott) who goes away with all the women's squads. She monitors the players' fitness levels at training camps and devises seasonal training programmes for them, which, as well as cardiovascular work, include regular weight-training sessions and plyometrics for strength and power. This makes our England fitness instructions in the 1970s (to 'go away and do your shuttle runs and make sure you turn up 100 per cent fit to play') look rather tame!

ENGLAND'S PROSPECTS FOR EURO 2005

So what impact has all this investment had on our performances in international competition? Where is the England team now in relation to its rivals and how can we expect to fare in Euro 2005?

The England women's team is currently (as of December 2004) ranked fourteenth in the FIFA world rankings. Our best finish in a major competition in recent times came back in 1995, when the team reached the semi-finals of the UEFA European Championships. At Euro 2001, England qualified for the finals but failed to progress from the group stages, losing to Sweden and Germany, who were the eventual finalists. England's best finish in the World Cup again came in 1995, when they reached the quarter-finals in Sweden. The team failed to qualify for the finals of subsequent competitions, which were won by the USA (1999) and Germany (2003).

So why are teams like Germany, Sweden and the USA currently outperforming us at senior level? One of the problems is that it is only comparatively recently (1993) that the FA took control of women's football in England and it was not until 1997/98 that the funding and the talent development structures required to develop a team that could compete with the best in the world began to be put in place. The top-ranked nations have had all these things for considerably longer and it has started to pay dividends for them. Germany (the current European and World Champions) for example, started later than us but from the inception of the national team in 1982, it was brought under Germany's governing body of football and was well funded and resourced with the aim of becoming a world leader. An Under-19 national team was introduced in 1990, followed by an Under-16 team in 1993.[9]

The story is similar with respect to double-Olympic and double-World Cup winners USA, and Sweden, who were runners-up in the World Cup in 2003 and came fourth in the 2004 Olympic Games. The Scandinavian countries and the USA also benefited from better equal opportunities policies in sport in the 1970s, which boosted female participation in football and saw women becoming top administrators and national coaches from far earlier than has been the case in England. Social attitudes towards women playing football in those countries have also been very different. Football has been seen as a sport for all and not primarily as 'a man's game'.

The situation in England has now improved. It is currently more acceptable for females to play football than it has been at any time in the past. With more opportunities for girls and women to participate in the game in schools, colleges and clubs, football has become the number one female participation sport.

We now have women in high positions in the FA (Kelly Simmons MBE, as head of national football development and Hope Powell OBE, as the women's national team coach). They are members of a small elite group of women who have been honoured by the Queen in recent years for services to women's football. Others include Sylvia Gore MBE and Sue Lopez MBE. There are also three women who now sit alongside the greats from men's football in the Hall of Fame at Preston Football Museum: Lily Parr of the Dick, Kerr Ladies team, Hope Powell and Sue Lopez, who both played for England. This reflects the growing status of the women's game in this country.

If the recent performances of the England youth teams are anything to go by, then the future does look promising for women's football at the elite level of the sport. England's Under-19 team reached the quarter-finals of the World Cup in Canada in 2002 and the semi-finals of the UEFA European championships in 2002 and 2003. Unfortunately, however, the team failed to reach the UEFA finals in 2004 and consequently missed out on the 2004 World Cup, which was won by Germany. The England Under-21 team was only set up in 2004; they have played one game to date against Sweden, which they won 1-0 away from home, a great start. At the moment, however, as far as the senior team goes, we are still playing catch-up. Of our opponents in the Euro 2005 finals (Germany, ranked first; Norway third; France fifth; Sweden sixth; Denmark seventh; Italy tenth and Finland sixteenth) only Finland is below England in the world rankings. On paper, therefore, England would not really be expected to progress beyond the group stages. The England team has, however, been drawn in what is arguably the weaker of the two groups (Group A) along with Sweden, Finland

and Denmark. Germany, the reigning World and European Champions, will be in Group B, joined by the strong Norway side, plus France and Italy. The top two teams in each group will progress to the semi-finals on 15 and 16 June.

Sweden and Denmark will be the favourites to go through from England's group but England beat Denmark 2-0 in 2004 and the team has had some good results in the build-up to Euro 2005, including a fantastic 4-1 victory over Italy, who are ranked four places higher, in February 2005. As the saying goes, 'anything can happen in football'. As the host nation England might just provide an upset!

In Kelly Smith (striker), Faye White (central defender) and Katy Chapman (a top midfielder, who plays for Charlton Athletic), England's team has a strong backbone of experienced, top-quality players, whose fitness and availability will be crucial to England's chances. England coach Hope Powell also has a good crop of young players that she can call upon, including strikers Emiola Aluko (Charlton Athletic), Amanda Barr and Karen Carney (both from Birmingham City). Barr and Carney both scored in the February win over Italy. It will be interesting to see how many of the youngsters make it into Hope's final squad of twenty.

The England team will begin its campaign on Sunday 5 June, against Finland at the City of Manchester Stadium, following the tournament's opening ceremony. The rest of England's group games will be played at Blackburn Rovers FC (against Denmark on 8 June and Sweden on 11 June). Matches at Euro 2005 will be going out live on Eurosport to fifty-four countries, which should provide a big showcase for the event. Games will also be shown on the BBC, which means that the championship will be brought to a much wider audience in this country than ever before. Bev Ward at the FA is also working hard behind the scenes to ensure that the national press are geared up to give good coverage to the matches, particularly those involving the England team.

THE EURO 2005 LEGACY

Whatever the outcome of the competition, hosting Euro 2005 is a very exciting prospect for women's football in England and the impact is likely to be felt for years to come. It has the potential to give a massive boost to female interest in the game in England, particularly in the North-West where the event is being staged. Other venues apart from those already mentioned include Preston North End, Blackpool FC and Warrington Wolves RLFC.

The FA is gearing itself up to take advantage of this and has planned a 'Legacy Programme' that will extend across the whole region. This involves putting money into the area beforehand in partnership with various other agencies (including the North-West Development Agency, Sport England

North West and the Government Office for the North-West) to make sure that everyone is ready with marketing packs and a range of activities including tournaments, festivals, conferences, coaching courses and road shows.[10] The intention is to capitalise on the event and get more girls and women involved in the game. This massive programme will be launched before Euro 2005 and will run for a year post-event, looking to link in with the Liverpool Capital of Culture Year of Sport 2006.

It will be an exciting time to be involved in women's football in the North-West. With events planned in nearby Warrington, Tranmere, Liverpool and Manchester, at Chester I will be close to the heart of things and will be looking to get involved in some of the activities that are being organised by the North-West Universities Association to promote the game in the region's higher education institutions.

FUTURE ISSUES FOR WOMEN'S FOOTBALL IN ENGLAND

But what does the future hold for women's football in England beyond the legacy of 2005? Without a crystal ball it is obviously difficult to say. In my opinion the game will continue growing at the grassroots level and it may be that its future in England is primarily as a participation sport. The FA is determined to continue working to boost the women's game at the elite end, however, and are applying to Sport England for money to develop the centres of excellence. According to Kelly Simmons, if they are successful in their January 2005 bid, the intention is to put £8 million into these centres over the following four years.

To ensure that there is a good structure in place to ensure the best possible future for club football in England, the FA is planning to introduce a 'Women's Pyramid of Football' in England over the next two years (2005-07). This will be a league system that will allow teams to be promoted or relegated from the FA Nationwide Women's Premier League at the top of the pyramid, through regional leagues, to County Leagues at its base.[11]

THE WORLD CUP 2007

The next big challenge for the England senior team after Euro 2005 will be to qualify for the 2007 World Cup Finals. I think that it is crucial that we don't miss out on the experience of playing in the finals of the most important competition in women's football for a third successive occasion. Hopefully Kelly Smith and Faye White will both be fit to play this time around. They were both out injured during the qualifying campaign for the 2003 World Cup where we were narrowly beaten by France in the play-offs. Over the next few years we should see more good young players from the successful England Under-19 and Under-21 teams coming through into the senior side and all the work being done at the National Player Development Centre will hopefully bear fruit.

It is still going to be almost impossible to match teams like the USA, however, in terms of depth of playing experience and preparation for major competitions. According to Kelly Smith, who studied, on a full soccer scholarship, at Seton Hall College in the USA and played in the professional women's league over there, the US players spent five months together in a full-time training camp before the last Olympics, during which time they were on salary. They also play about 20-25 games a year, which means that they have players who have accumulated 80 to 100 caps in a relatively short space of time. To all intents and purposes the USA team is professional and, while the England team retains its essentially amateur status, it is going to be difficult to match the world leaders in the game.

AMATEURISM v. PROFESSIONALISM

The amateur/professional issue is also one that is going to be to the fore in relation to the development of club football in this country during the coming years. It will be interesting to see whether or not the FA introduces a professional women's league at some time in the future. This was something that was mooted back in 2001, when the FA employed Karen Doyle as head of women's football (marketing and commercial) to carry out a two-year feasibility study. This concluded that the time was not yet right for a professional league to prosper in England. It was felt that the main ingredients for success, such as funding, spectatorship, facilities, qualified coaches and a talent pool of players, were not yet at an adequate level to support it.[12] One professional men's football club (Fulham FC, the club that I supported in the late 1960s) did fund the first ever professional women's team in this country for three seasons between 2000 and 2003. They signed international players from England and overseas and were successful in winning the domestic treble (League, League Cup and FA Cup) in the 2002/03 season. When a professional women's league did not take off, however, the funding to pay the Fulham players as full-time professionals was withdrawn. Many of the top players, such as England trio Katie Chapman, Rachel Yankey and Rachel Unitt subsequently left to join other clubs and although the team was still in the National Division of the FA Women's Premier League in the 2004/05 season, it had slipped right out of contention with those at the top of the league.

The idea of a professional women's league has not been completely abandoned, however, although there are no plans to introduce one in the immediate future. Bev Ward at the FA told me that the governing body still wants it to happen when the women's game in this country reaches the appropriate stage in its development to make it viable. Given the recent demise of the world's first professional women's soccer league in the USA (WUSA), the FA's decision to hang fire is probably a very wise one. With sport in general and women's football in particular being just about as popular and successful over there as anywhere else in the world, you could say that if the game didn't take off as a professional sport in the USA then it certainly won't in England. This could be true but, according to Kelly Smith, the problems experienced in the USA were a product of trying to make the pro-league 'as big as possible as soon as possible, instead of working up slowly'. It was set up in 2001 'in a blaze of fireworks' following the national team's success in winning the 1999 World Cup (hosted by the USA). Each of the eight teams in the league was owned by a cable TV company but TV audiences and attendances at matches were not big enough to support expenditure. The twenty-two players from the US national team that won the World Cup were spread out across the eight teams and apparently paid as much as $85,000 a year. By 2003, in only its third season of operation and despite the players taking sizeable pay cuts, the financial situation had reached a critical level and the league suspended operations only a few days before the 2003 World Cup was due to kick off in the USA. Efforts are now being made to get the league up and running again for the 2005 season, based this time on a more sound business plan.

The failure of 'the USA experiment' may not therefore mean that there is no future for professional women's football in England. The FA's more cautious approach to the issue in this country may indeed pay off in the long run. In the meantime most of the teams in the National Division of the FA Women's Premier League, which in the 2004/05 season included Arsenal, Charlton Athletic, Leeds United, Birmingham City, Fulham, Bristol Rovers, Everton, Liverpool, Bristol City and Doncaster Rovers Belles, have links with their professional men's club, which is something that the FA has been keen to encourage, although the nature of the support that they enjoy varies a great deal. Arsenal Ladies, for instance, are fully integrated into Arsenal Football Club and are funded by them. Faye White is one of six or seven players who are employed by the club. She assists in the running of Arsenal Ladies FC and works as a coach delivering sessions to girls in the Greater London area. Other players are paid to assist at Arsenal Football Club's Academy or Centre of Excellence for girls. While some of the other women's teams have similar set-ups, others get little more from their professional men's club than some help with the provision of the team kit. Some of the top women's teams have also begun to give players some sort of financial inducement to play (such as payment per game, or win bonuses) but again this varies from club to club.

While clubs like Arsenal Ladies are obviously benefiting from their association with a top men's professional club, there are downsides to the arrangement.

Arsenal Ladies don't actually have their own pitch. They have used Highbury on occasions but play most of their home games at Boreham Wood FC, which is a men's football club. According to Faye White, Arsenal Ladies' matches get cancelled if the men's team needs the pitch for Sunday fixtures, or if it is felt that the women's match would mess up the pitch. This is a common problem in women's football and one that contributed to the FA's decision to hang fire on the introduction of a professional women's league. An uncertain or changeable fixture list is not a good basis for ensuring the type of attendance figures at matches that would be necessary to support it. As a woman who started playing football in the 1960s, when women were banned from playing on league grounds, I would actually advise women's football clubs to be cautious about relying too heavily on the patronage of the men's clubs to ensure their future. One day, when it doesn't suit their purpose or women's football becomes too popular and is seen as a threat to the men's game, they might just take it away. It happened to Dick, Kerr Ladies back in the 1920s; is there any reason to believe that it couldn't happen again?

MEDIA COVERAGE

Another issue related to the amateurism versus professionalism debate in women's football is that of media coverage. If the game is going to attract the sort of crowds and sponsorship that will be necessary to make a professional women's league viable in the future, then the sport is going to need to become far more high profile in the media than it is currently. The content and the extent of coverage both in the national press and on television has improved considerably since I was playing for England in the 1970s. Current reports tend to focus on fixtures, results and football action rather than on the players' appearance and what boyfriends think about them playing such an unladylike sport! It is still the case, however, that you need to know exactly where and when to look to find any coverage; if you blink you might miss it!

This relatively low profile has consequences for the women's game beyond the professionalism question. It also means that young girls are still struggling to find elite female playing role models that they can identify with. This was brought home to me recently, in May 2004, in conversation with some of the girls from the Sport Cheshire Advanced Coaching Centre at University College Chester. I was chatting to the under-twelves at the end-of-season tournament and asked them who their playing heroes/heroines were. Coming from the Merseyside area, needless to say they all named players who were at that time playing for either Liverpool (like Michael Owen and Steven Gerrard) or Everton (such as Wayne Rooney). When I asked them if there were any female players that they admired, their faces were blank. I went on to see if they could name any of the top female club players or members of the England women's football team. None of them could!

This is something that obviously needs to be addressed. The FA is working hard to improve media coverage and information dissemination with respect to women's football. It has a marketing and communications strategy for the women's game that has included encouraging journalists to cover games; getting the results on Teletext on a Sunday and trying to get matches shown on the television.[13] In the 2003/04 season, five games were shown on Sky and the Women's FA Cup final was transmitted live on BBC1, attracting an audience of 2.2 million. Four national newspapers currently cover women's football on a weekly basis. This amounts to a column in the *Guardian* and the *Daily Express*, a 300-word preview in the *Sunday Mirror* and a news story in *The Times* on a Monday.[14] This represents a great improvement on the situation that existed as recently as three or four years ago. Compared to the pages and pages of coverage devoted to men's football in every tabloid and broadsheet on every day of the week, it is still a drop in the ocean, however, and, as I commented previously, if you don't know when and where to look for the few reports that are written on the women's game, they are easily missed.

For the serious fan it is, however, far easier to access information on women's football now than it has ever been in the past. As well as a specialist magazine that can be subscribed to (*Fair Game*) a wealth of information is accessible via the internet. The FA, UEFA and FIFA websites now provide up-to-the-minute information on women's football from around the world. Most of the top clubs also have their own websites (Arsenal Ladies' website is linked up to the men's). In addition to this there are literally dozens of other sites covering all aspects of the game from playing, coaching and refereeing, to spectatorship and the history of the game.

People are not likely to search out this information, however, unless they already have an interest in the sport. In order to increase participation and spectatorship in women's football in this country, raising the profile of the game in the press and broadcast media is still going to be very important for the future. Young girls need some female icons to look up to and the media has the power to create them. There are plenty of candidates in the current England squad and it would be wonderful to see them gain star status in the future to equal that of some of the all-time greats from the USA team, such as Mia Hamm and Brandi Chastain. They might need to do something really exceptional to achieve this, however, like win the World Cup for England in front of a capacity crowd in the new Wembley Stadium! This may seem like an impossible task, but if I could go back to the future, as a young England player, that is what I would be dreaming of!

HIGHER EDUCATION AND WOMEN'S FOOTBALL

For this dream to have a chance of coming true, we are going to have to match our competitors in terms of preparation. Teams like the USA not only benefit from bringing the national squad together for extended periods before a major tournament but also from the fact that many of the players live, train and play together all the year round within a college system that is highly professional and produces both elite players and coaches for the sport. The National Player Development Centre at Loughborough is an attempt to try to address this issue and should pay big dividends in future years. There is also, in my opinion, huge potential to develop women's football right across the higher education sector in this country where sports facilities, residential accommodation and courses in sport and exercise science abound.

A growing number of institutions are currently investing (or have imminent plans to invest) in the improvement of their sports facilities, are appointing directors of sport and putting into place strategies aimed at both increasing participation and supporting elite sport. Three-quarters of institutions, for instance, now offer sports bursaries to elite performers.[15] This overall trend was recently identified by Sport England[16] who now recognises the sector's potential and in 2004 stated its intention to raise the profile of higher education and sport.

With the Government aiming to get fifty per cent of young people aged eighteen to thirty into higher education, this represents a big potential talent pool of bright young females that could provide the players, coaches and development managers for women's football in the future. As an ex-England international, coach to a university college women's football team, an FA coach educator and a senior lecturer in sport and exercise science, this type of performance initiative (aimed at raising the standard and profile of women's football in the higher education sector) is one that I would love to be involved with in the next phase of my career. All that I can say about this at the moment however is watch this space!

Notes

ONE: GETTING STARTED

1 Information extracted from the *WFA Mitre Cup final Programme*, 1973.
2 Lopez, S. *Women on the Ball: A Guide to Women's Football*. London: Scarlett Press (1997).

TWO: HITTING THE BIG TIME

1 Lopez, S. *Women on the Ball: A Guide to Women's Football*. London: Scarlett Press (1997).
2 Lopez, S. *Women on the Ball: A Guide to Women's Football*. London: Scarlett Press (1997).
3 Information extracted from the *Mitre Cup final Programme*, 1972.
4 Information extracted from the *Mitre Cup final Programme*, 1972.
5 Information on Southampton's playing record gleaned from Lopez, S. *Women on the Ball: A Guide to Women's Football*. London: Scarlett Press (1997).
6 Lopez, S. *Women on the Ball: A Guide to Women's Football*. London: Scarlett Press (1997).
7 Lopez, S. *Women on the Ball: A Guide to Women's Football*. London: Scarlett Press (1997).
8 Information supplied by Patricia Gregory (former secretary of the WFA), 2004.
9 Lopez, S. *Women on the Ball: A Guide to Women's Football*. London: Scarlett Press (1997).

SIX: COACHING FOOTBALL IN ENGLAND (1973-1992)

1 Information on Dartford's early curriculum gleaned from
   www.greenwichalumni.co.uk/bou/mbo.htm, 18/10/2004.
2 *Mitre Cup final Programme*, 1974.
3 *Pony WFA Cup final Programme*, 1978.

SEVEN: A NEW ERA

1 From information supplied by Kelly Simmons, FA head of national football development, 2004.
2 From information supplied by Rachel Pavlou, FA regional development manager, 2004.
3 Football Association Coaches' Association (2000). *Membership details*, in Williams, J. *A Game for Rough Girls? A History of Women's Football in Britain*. London: Routledge (2003).
4 From information supplied by Kelly Simmons, FA head of football development, 2004.
5 From information provided by Stewart Fowlie, BUSA sports programme manager, 2004.
6 From information supplied by Donna McIvor, FA national development manager (Education), 2005.

EIGHT: BACK TO THE FUTURE

1 From the *WFA Mitre Cup final programme*,1973.
2 From information supplied by Kelly Simmons, FA head of national football
  development, 2004.
3 Football Association Coaches' Association (2000). *Membership details*, in Williams, J.
  A Game for Rough Girls? A History of Women's Football in Britain. London: Routledge
  (2003).
4 From information supplied by Stewart Fowlie, BUSA sports programme manager, 2004.
5 From information supplied by Kelly Simmons, FA head of national football
  development, 2004.
6 From information supplied by Kelly Simmons, FA head of national football
  development, 2004.
7 From information supplied by Bev Ward, FA marketing manager for women's football,
  2004.
8 From information supplied by Patricia Gregory (former secretary of the WFA), 2005.
9 Lopez, S. *Women on the Ball: A Guide to Women's Football*. London: Scarlett Press (1997).
10 From information supplied by Kelly Simmons, FA national head of football
  development, 2004.
11 From information supplied by Kelly Simmons, FA national head of football
  development, 2004.
12 From information supplied by Bev Ward, FA marketing manager for women's football,
  2004.
13 From information supplied by Bev Ward, FA marketing manager for women's football,
  2004.
14 From information supplied by Bev Ward, FA marketing manager for women's football,
  2004.
15 Sport England. *Higher Education and Sport in England: Executive Summary*. London: Sport
  England (2004).
16 Sport England. *Higher Education and Sport in England: Executive Summary*. London: Sport
  England (2004).

International Playing Career

DATE	COMPETITION	VERSUS	VENUE	SCORE
18.11.72★	Friendly	Scotland	Greenock, Ravenscraig Stadium	Won 3-2
22.04.73	Friendly	France	Brion, Brion Stadium	Won 3-0
23.06.73	Friendly	Scotland	Nuneaton Borough Fc	Won 8-0
7.9.73	Friendly	N. Ireland	Bath City FC	won 5-1
9.11.73	Friendly	Netherlands	Reading FC, Elm Park	Won 1-0
17.3.74	Friendly	Wales	Slough Town FC	Won 5-0
31.5.74	Friendly	Netherlands	Groningen, Stadspark Stadium	Won 3-0
7.11.74	Friendly	France	Wimbledon FC, Plough Lane	Won 2-0
19.4.75	Friendly	Switzerland	Basle, Schutzenmatte Stadium	Won 3-1
15.6.75	Friendly	Sweden	Gothenburg, Ullevi Stadium	Lost 2-0
7.9.75	Friendly	Sweden	Wimbledon FC, Plough Lane	Lost 3-1
2.5.76★	Friendly	Netherlands	Blackpool RFC, Borough Park	Won 2-1
22.5.76	Home International	Wales	Bedford Town FC	Won 4-0
23.5.76	Home International	Scotland	Enfield FC	Won 5-1
2.6.76	Friendly	Italy	Rome, Olympic Stadium	Lost 2-0
5.6.76	Friendly	Italy	Cesena	Lost 2-1
17.10.76	Friendly	Wales	Ebbw Vale, Eugene Cross Welfare Ground	Won 2-1
26.2.77	Friendly	France	Paris	Drew 0-0

★ denotes substitute appearance

Key Dates in Women's Football in the post-1966 era

1967   First Deal International Tournament; organised by Arthur Hobbs.

1969   First Butlin's Cup competition staged; winners are Foden Ladies.
Women's Football Association (WFA) formed with forty-four clubs.

1970   January: FA rescinds 1921 ban and allows women access to affiliated pitches and referees.
April: Southampton Ladies play Manchester Corinthians at Empire Pool, Wembley with the backing of the CCPR and the FA.
June: Seven leagues in operation under the WFA.

1971   First WFA Mitre Cup final, Crystal Palace National Recreation Centre; winners are Southampton.
Unofficial 'World Cup' held in Mexico; winners are Denmark.
100 clubs affiliated to the WFA.
UEFA directs national associations in its member nations to recognise women's football and take steps to see that it is properly controlled.

1972   February: FA recognises the WFA as the governing body of women's football in England at that time.
18 November: First official women's international match in Britain; Greenock in Scotland; England beat Scotland 3-2; scorer of first England goal is Sylvia Gore.

1973   April: *WFA Cup final Programme* records that there are 300 registered clubs in England, over twenty leagues and approximately 5,000 players.
June: First England team home match (Nuneaton); England beat Scotland 8-0; first player to score a hat-trick for England is Pat Firth.
September: First England match under floodlights, Twerton Park, Bath; England beat Northern Ireland 5-1.
November: First England match on a Football League ground, Elm Park, Reading; England beat Holland 1-0.

1975   First England defeat: Sweden 2 England 0; Gothenburg.

1976   May: Inaugural Home International Championship; winners are England.

1983   WFA invited to affiliate to FA and given County FA status.

1984   First European Championships: England reach the final against Sweden and draw 1-1; Sweden win on penalties.

1991   First FIFA Women's World Cup, China: winners USA; England did not take part.
           First WFA National League competition.

1993   FA take control of women's football in England.
           First match under FA. Slovenia 10 England 0 (away).

1994   First FA Women's Challenge Cup final.
           FA Women's Premier League replaces WFA National League.

1995   Euro 1995: England reach the semi-finals (best finish to date).
           Second Women's World Cup, Sweden: England reach quarter-finals; winners are Norway.

1997   England Under-16 and Under-18 teams established.
           First UEFA Under-18 Championships.
           FA launches Talent Development Plan for Women's Football.

1998   Hope Powell appointed as the first full-time national coach of an England women's team.
           First FA Centres of Excellence for females launched.

1999   USA win third Women's World Cup, USA; England fail to qualify.
           187 teams enter FA Women's Challenge Cup.

2000   Start of Active Sports Programme (Five-year programme), which provides £8 million partnership funding for women's football.

2001   UEFA European Women's Championships: England reach the finals but lose in the group stage to Sweden and Germany (eventual finalists).
           FA National Player Development Centre takes in first intake.
           UEFA change international team age groups to under-seventeen and under-nineteen.
           4,500 registered teams in England.

2002   England Under-19s get to quarter-finals of World Cup in Canada.
           In the 2001/02 season, football became the top participation sport for females in England.
           BBC televise the FA Women's Cup final (2.5 million viewers).

2003   Germany win fourth Women's World Cup, USA: England fail to qualify for the finals.

2003/04   6,000 girls' teams and 1,000 women's teams in England. The number of females playing the game for registered clubs breaks the 100,000 mark.

2004/05   Fifty-one licensed FA Centres of Excellence for females in England.

2004/05   England Under-21 team set up.

2005   Sixth UEFA European Women's Championships (England qualify as hosts).

Index

Active Sports Programme 128, 129, 138
Adams, John 53, 54, 55, 58, 67
AIAW (Association of Intercollegiate
    Athletics for Women)
    first National Championship 92, 94
Aikin, Gladys 39, 69
Aston Villa 30
Allott, Jeannie 47, 48, 68, 71
Arsenal Ladies FC 139, 145, 146, 147
Atkinson, Ron 26, 27

Badrock, Elaine 61, 65
Bagguley, Janet 47, 48, 71
Bampton, Debbie 67
Belmont Abbey College, North Carolina
    82, 83-84
Bennett, Theresa 115
Best, George 13, 85, 89
Bilton, Flo 68, 137
Bisham Abbey 44, 46, 59
Brunton (née Manning), Julia 45, 54
Bruton, Jenny 69
Bruton, John 69
Buckett, Sue 46, 56, 106
BUSA (British Universities Sports
    Association)
    FA support of 132-133
    men's championship
        Chester College results (1998/99)
        125, 126
    women's championship
        birth and growth of 118, 130, 136
        Chester College results (2000-04)
        130-131
Butlin's Cup (1970) 20-25

Cannon, Ed 93
Channon, Mick 45, 73
Chapman, Katy 142
Chapman, Pat 62, 106, 107
Chastain, Brandi 147
Chester City Football Club 122, 123,
    133
Chester College
    women's football team, 1987-88 116-
        118
    2000-04 130-132
    men's football team 125-126
Choat, Sandra 60, 74
Clifford (née Lee), Josie 127
Coffin, Linda 62
Cooper, Jacci 120, 123
Corderoy, Sue 29
Croker, Ted 74, 115
Crystal Palace 27, 29, 30

Daily Express National Five-a-Side
    Championship 44-46
Dartford College 37, 41
    women's football team 77, 102-108
    1976/77 WFA Cup quarter-final 82,
        105-108
Davies, Pat 46, 50, 54, 56, 74, 106
De La Salle College 116, 134
Deal International Tournament 30, 35
Deal Town 30
Deighan, Liz 60
Dick, Kerr Ladies 17, 23, 141, 146
Dorrance, Anson 94
Dunne, Fay 122

Edwards, Louise 121, 123
Ebben Roger 39
England women's team
    achievements 67, 137, 140, 142
    coaching 46, 47, 120, 138, 139
    first official international match 50-52
    first match on a professional league
        ground 59
    first match under floodlights 58
    first player to gain 50 caps 60
    fitness training 53, 54, 140
    funding of 63, 64, 69, 138-140
    kit 45, 63, 140
    media coverage 44, 47, 48, 59, 63, 70-
        74, 137, 142, 146-147
    staffing levels 67, 140
    sports science support 138, 140
    Pony Home International
        Championship 62-64, 73
    trials 36-41
    Under-15 team 137
    Under-17 team 137
    Under-19 team 141
    Under-21 team 141
Evans, Michelle 122

FA (Football Association)
    academies 133, 137, 138
    Active Sports Programme 128, 129,
        138
    attitude towards women's football in the
        1980s 115-116
    ban on women's use of affiliated pitches
        17, 72
        effect of ban 17
        lifting of ban 19, 72
    Centres of Excellence for girls 120,
        129, 133, 137, 138, 143
    coaching centres for girls 128-130
    grassroots development of girls' football
        119-120
    first woman to be reported to FA 25
    Head of women's football 119, 120
    marketing and communications strategy
        143, 144, 147
    National Coach 120, 138, 141
    National Division of the Women's
        Premier League 121, 144, 145-146
    National Player Development Centre
        137, 138, 144, 148
    number of affiliated female teams 136-
        137
    number of registered female players 138
    number of qualified female coaches 136
    takes over from the WFA 119
        talent development initiatives 120,
            122, 128, 129, 137, 140, 143, 144,
            148
Firth, Pat 56, 61
Fish, Sue 23
Foden Ladies 23, 25-27, 30, 39, 47
Foreman, Eileen 54, 56
Fort Lauderdale Strikers 81, 89, 90
France
    matches against England 53-55, 60, 66,
        73
Francis, Gerry 73
Fulham Football Club
    Craven Cottage 12, 13, 88

German Women's National team
    achievements 137, 140, 141, 142
    organisation 137, 140-141
Gibson, Betty 69
Gore Sylvia 23, 26, 27, 121, 122, 123, 130,
    141
Gregg, Lauren 94
Gregory, Patricia 48, 68, 137

Hale, Lynda 46, 106, 107
Hamm, Mia 101, 147
Heskey, Emile 122, 123
Higher Education Sector
    current status of women's football 130,
        132-133
    potential for future contribution to
        women's football 133, 148
Hill, Gordon 80, 81, 82, 83, 84, 90, 91
Hobbs, Arthur 35, 68, 137
Howard, Roley 75, 76
Hundred of Hoo School 81, 108-110,
    114
Hunt, David 69, 137
Hurst, Geoff 12, 45
Hyde, Ron 69

Italy
    matches against England 64-66, 67,
        137, 142

Jaycocks, June 69, 137
Johnstone, John 104

Kaufman, Jim 92, 94, 95, 97
Keeley, Graham 126
Kirkland, Maggie (see Pearce)
Kuhlmann, Jim 92, 93, 95, 96

Leagues
    Home Counties League 27, 28, 29, 37
    Midlands League 29
    Oxfordshire League 18
    South Bucks Youth Clubs League 17
Lee, Jose (see Clifford)
Leeds United 13,14
Lees Ladies (formerly Stewarton and
    Thistle) 30, 31, 32
Leicester EMGALS 27, 30, 31, 32
Leyland, Kelly 122
Lopez, Sue 55, 58, 74, 82, 106, 122, 141
Los Angeles Aztecs 81
Loughborough University 37, 40, 131,
    134, 138, 148

Madame Osterberg 102, 103, 108
Manning, Julia (see Brunton)
Manchester Corinthians 23, 35
Marcos, Francisco 75, 76, 77, 79, 80, 85,
    86, 87
Marlowe, David 69, 72, 137
Marsh, Rodney 81, 85, 86, 89, 90, 91, 92
McCune, Carole (see Thomas)
McDougall, Kelly 122
McGroarty, Margaret (Paddy) 21, 28, 30,
    36, 37, 39, 47, 48, 56, 62, 68, 71
McIvor, Donna 133
Media coverage of women's football 22,
    33, 47, 48, 59, 63, 70-74, 81, 105, 146,
    147
Miks, Maggie 56
Miley, Fiona 117, 118
Mimms, Bobby 127
Murphy, Colin 112, 113

NASL (North American Soccer League)
    offside rule 89
    penalty shoot-out rules 90
    Soccer Bowl Finals 1975 80-81
                  1978 90-91
                  1979 91-92

Netherlands
    matches against England 59-60, 73
New York Cosmos 85, 90, 95
Northern Ireland
    matches against England 58, 62
Norway 15, 62, 137, 141, 142

Owen, Claire 122
Owen, Wendy
    at Beaconsfield Youth Club 17
    at Carnegie 113-116
    at Dartford College 41, 43, 77, 82, 102-
        108
    at De La Salle College 116
    at Hartwick College, Oneonta, USA
        75-80
    at the Hundred of Hoo School 108-
        110
    at The Soccer Farm, USA 91-100
    at Sport Cheshire Advanced Coaching
        Centre 128-130
    at Thame Ladies 20-36
    at Tampa Bay Rowdies, Florida, USA
        80-91
    at Tranmere Rovers Centre of
        Excellence 120-122
    at University College Chester 116-118,
        125-126, 128-135
    birth and early life 11-19
    brothers' influence 15
    debut for England 50, 53-55
    England trials 36-41
    England appearances 44-67
    expectations for Euro 2005 140-142
    family background 11
    father's influence 12, 16, 17
    injury 66-67
    meeting Michael Owen 122-124
    obsession with football 12, 16
    on FA Coaching Award courses
    FA Preliminary Coaching Certificate
        110-112
    FA Preparatory Course 112-113
    UEFA 'B' Licence 124-126
    UEFA 'A' Licence 126-128
    on playing for England in the 1970s
        compared to the present 137, 138-
        140
    on the future of the modern game
        143-148

picked for first England squad 41
press coverage 70-74, 146-147
retirement as an England player 66
role models 13
school years 12, 16
work as a Coach Educator 133-135
Owen, Michael 122, 123, 124, 146

Parker, Sheila 23, 47, 54, 56, 60, 62, 74
Pavlou, Rachel 119
Pearson (née Kirkland), Maggie 46, 47, 56, 106
Pearson, Nigel 127
Pele 85, 91
Pemberton, John 127
Pomfret School, Connecticut 92, 95
Powell, Hope 138, 140, 141, 142
Professionalism in women's football 133, 139, 144-146, 148

Quraishi, Farrukh 79

Role models 13, 21, 76, 79, 97, 128, 132, 146
Russell, Robin 112

Scotland
    Matches against England 45-52, 55-58, 62-63, 70
Sex Discrimination Act (1975) 87, 115
School football for girls 12, 16, 18, 82, 87, 95, 100, 102, 104, 108, 109, 110, 114, 115, 118, 119, 120, 129, 135, 138, 141
Scheuber, Helen 122
Simmons, Kelly 119, 120, 129, 141, 143
Smith, Graham 121
Smith, Kelly 138, 139, 142, 143, 144, 145
Soccer Farm
    coaching staff 93-95
Sport Cheshire Advanced Coaching Centre 128-130
Stewarton and Thistle (later Lees Ladies) 30, 31, 32
Southampton Ladies 27, 30, 31, 32, 35, 37, 39, 46, 47, 58, 62
Suckling, Perry 127
Sweden
    matches against England 61-62, 67, 137, 140, 141, 142

organisation of women's football 62, 137, 140, 141
social attitudes towards women's football 141
Switzerland
    matches against England 60-61

Talbot, Jane 67
Tampa Bay Rowdies
    Community Relations Programme 85-86
    Kamp Kick in the Grass 81, 82, 84, 85
    marketing strategy 84-85
    press conferences 86-87
    Soccer Bowl, 1978 90-91
Taylor, Ernie 67
Taylor, Jody 122
Thame Gazette 22, 35
Thame Ladies team
    1970 Butlins Cup Final 23
    1970/71 season 25-27
    1971/72 season 27-35
    1972 Home Counties League Cup Final 29
    1972 WFA Cup semi-final 30
    1972 WFA Cup losing semi-finalists play-off 31
    1972 France Trip 33-34
    changing facilities 32-36
    funding 27
    management 28, 35, 36
    matches against Fodens 23, 25-26, 30
    matches against Southampton 30
    media coverage of 20, 22, 23, 25, 32, 33, 35
    medical support 33
    players 20, 21, 30
    socialising 28
    supporters 22
    training 23, 25
Thomas (née McCune), Carol 60, 62, 68
Title 1X 87
Tranmere Rovers' Centre of Excellence 120, 121, 122, 128, 129, 130
Tranter, Tommy 58, 59, 67

UEFA women's championships 137, 140, 141
    Euro 2005
        teams and rankings 136, 140-142

England's prospects 140–142
England team preparations 139, 142
Legacy Programme 142–143
venues 142
UK Elite 132, 134, 135
University of North Carolina 94
Unitt, Rachel 144
Unofficial World Cup (1971) 26
USA
attitude towards female soccer players
and coaches 80, 84, 85, 86, 87, 90
collegiate women's soccer 75, 78, 87,
92, 93, 94, 100, 116, 133, 144, 148
female role models 94, 101, 147
growth of women's soccer 75, 78, 81,
87, 90, 92, 94, 95, 100–101, 116, 135,
141, 144, 145
national women's team 75, 94, 100,
101, 135, 140, 141, 144, 145, 147,
148
sports spectatorship in the USA and
England, compared 88–89
women's professional soccer league
(WUSA) 139, 145
women's soccer in the USA and
England compared 75, 86–87, 95,
116, 133, 135, 140, 141, 144, 145,
148

Wales
matches against England 58, 62, 63, 66

Ward, Bev 139, 142, 144
Wembley Stadium 44–45, 70, 147
Westhorn United 47
WFA Cup 30, 31, 32, 35, 82, 104, 105,
108, 139
WFA Mitre Cup 27, 29, 30, 31, 32, 35
WFA (Women's Football Asssociation)
formation 19
funding 36, 139
number of affiliated clubs 19, 27, 72
Preliminary Coaching Certificate 75,
77, 82, 110–111
Whelan, Fern 122
White, Faye 138, 140, 142, 143, 145, 146
Wilcox, Dan 93
Wilder, Sandy 93
Woog, Dan 94
Woolpit Bluebirds 21, 40
World Cup (men's)
1966 12, 13, 14, 17
World Cup (women's)
1991 67, 101
1995 67, 140
1999 140, 145
2003 140, 141, 143, 145
Worthington, Eric 37, 39, 40, 73

Yankey, Rachel 144
Yallop, Richard 75

Other titles published by Tempus

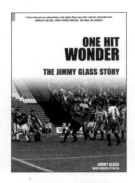

One Hit Wonder The Jimmy Glass Story
JIMMY GLASS WITH ROGER LYTOLLIS

Incredibly, it was on-loan goalkeeper Jimmy Glass's 95th-minute goal in the last game of the 1998/99 season that kept Carlisle in the Football League. His career spanned every level of the game and saw him battling to stay afloat in a sport awash with money but drowning in debt. A world away from the standard football biography, this amazingly honest account gives the inside story of the most dramatic period of change the sport has ever seen.
0 7524 3181 1

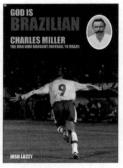

God is Brazilian Charles Miller, the Man Who Brought Football to Brazil
JOSH LACEY

In 1894, Charles Miller arrived in Brazil with a football. When he reached São Paulo, he was shocked to discover that no one knew how to play. So he marked out a pitch, gathered twenty young men, and divided them into two teams… Today, Brazil is the greatest footballing nation in the world, and Miller has been forgotten. This is his story – a gripping narrative of one man's love of football and the clash between two very different cultures.
0 7524 3414 4

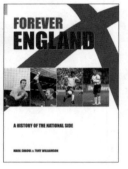

Forever England A History of the National Side
MARK SHAOUL & TONY WILLIAMSON

This insightful and fascinating account, which covers the careers of England's all-time great players and the team's successes, failures and near misses, is an essential read for anyone interested in the history of the three lions. From the amateur gentlemen of the 1870s to the stars of the early twenty-first century, with many wonderfully evocative illustrations, it is the definitive history of England's national football team.
0 7524 2939 6

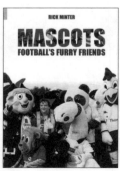

Mascots Football's Furry Friends
RICK MINTER

Meet the mascots in this remarkable illustrated guide. It reveals a crazy and colourful world of glamour, fun, and rivalry, where football's pecking order works in reverse! Follow the remarkable story of Cyril the Swan (the eight foot rascal at Swansea), relive the tale of H'Angus (Hartlepool's monkey mascot who sensationally got elected as Mayor) and see the capers of Yorkie, the king of the jungle who fought to save York City.
0 7524 3179 X

If you are interested in purchasing other books published by Tempus, or in case you have difficulty finding any Tempus books in your local bookshop, you can also place orders directly through our website
www.tempus-publishing.com